MASTERING MULTIFAMILY UNDERWRITING

5 STEPS TO CONFIDENT, RISK-SMART APARTMENT INVESTING

VESSI KAPOULIAN

Disclaimer

The content in the book represents the views, opinions, and experiences of the author and is not intended to serve as individual tax, legal, financial, or investment advice.

DEDICATION

To my mother, **Rossi Kapulyan:**

You taught me to dream big, to believe in myself, and to pursue my goals with determination. You have always been by my side, showing me what unconditional love looks like and what it means to be a great mom. You are my guiding light, my heart, my everything. Love you to the Moon and Sun and back infinite times. This book is as much yours as it is mine.

TABLE OF CONTENTS

INSIDER'S KIT

To access the complimentary resources that accompany this book, go to: www.MasteringMultifamilyUnderwriting.com/book-resources.

For additional guidance on multifamily underwriting, go here: www.MasteringMultifamilyUnderwriting.com

"The essence of investment management is the management of risks, not the management of returns."

- Benjamin Graham

INTRODUCTION

I am Vessi Kapoulian.

A former commercial lender and risk manager. I was responsible for managing a $1BN+ credit portfolio and have transacted on more than $500MM in real estate. Over the years I have underwritten more than 1,000 multifamily deals. Today, I am both an active multifamily investor and a due diligence adviser to investors and family offices.

But here is what you may not expect: I was not born knowing how to underwrite.

When I first began, underwriting felt overwhelming. The "science" was intimidating with its formulas and acronyms, while the "art" of balancing assumptions and judgment seemed slippery and subjective. If you have ever stared at a spreadsheet and felt like giving up, you are not alone. I have been there too.

And yet, this is where many investors stop. Overwhelmed by the data and numbers, they look for the 'Easy' button and rely on glossy pitch decks, celebrity operators, or friends' endorsements. Too often, that ends in disappointment. I have witnessed it firsthand—in calls with passive investors dealing with capital calls, failed partnerships, or distressed assets. I have seen the same five reasons why deals fail surface again and again: aggressive underwriting, lack of operational discipline, mismatch between the debt and the business plan, thin capitalization, and failed partnerships.

I wrote this book during a period when I watched too many good people lose money on bad deals—not because they were not smart, but because they did not have the right tools.

And while I cannot prevent every bad deal in the marketplace, what I can do is help limit how far that pain spreads through the power of education. This book is my way of sharing the lessons I learned—sometimes painfully—so you can avoid repeating them. My goal is to help you underwrite with clarity, confidence, and ease, no matter your starting point.

If you are reading this, you are already ahead of 90% of investors. You are choosing education over excitement, process over promises. That choice will serve you well.

This is not about becoming a professional underwriter. It is about never again having to trust blindly when your financial future is on the line.

Your journey starts now.

Vessi Kapoulian

THE BELIEFS THAT HOLD YOU BACK

Perhaps as you pick up this book, you are already hearing doubts in your head:

- *"I am not an underwriter."* Neither was I. No one is born knowing how to analyze a deal. This book breaks it all down in plain English and gives you a step-by-step, repeatable process.

- *"What if I still miss something?"* That is always possible, which is why I show you how to build your own checklist. Even today, I use one—just like a pilot does before every flight.

- *"I have never done this before."* Perfect. This book was designed for you. If you are new to multifamily, you will see that within weeks of practice you can analyze deals from A to Z.

- *"Underwriting is too complex."* Not when it is broken into clear, repeatable steps. Complexity turns into confidence with practice.

- *"I do not have time."* Each chapter can stand on its own, meeting you where you are. You can move at your own pace and refer back to it if and as needed.

- *"There are no good deals in this market."* There is never a perfect time. The worst time to start learning is when a deal is already sitting in your inbox. The best time is now. Start learning now, to avoid costly mistakes later.

HOW THIS BOOK WORKS

To guide you, I have built this book around a character named **Jane Morgan**. Jane begins as many readers do—eager to invest, but uncertain about the numbers. Through her journey, she transforms into a savvy, confident investor.

Jane's story is fictional, but the lessons are not. Every story, every case study, every pitfall, and every turnaround you will read here is based on real deals I have underwritten or reviewed. Identifying details have been removed to protect confidentiality, but the patterns are authentic.

The book itself follows a clear structure:

1. **The Foreclosure Email** (Chapter 1) – Jane's painful wake-up call and the day everything changes.

2. **The Core Lessons** (Chapters 2-5) – Understanding multifamily assets, myths, markets, and key financial concepts.

3. **The Five-Step Framework** (Chapter 6) – A repeatable underwriting process covering income, expenses, reserves, debt, and valuation.

4. **Case Studies** (Chapters 7-8) – Real-world examples and tools that bring the framework to life.

5. **The Lender's Perspective** (Chapter 9) – How banks think and what questions to ask.

6. **Fees, Waterfalls, and Key PPM Sections** (Chapter 10) – Understanding common waterfall structures and key areas of the Private Placement Memorandum (PPM) to pay attention to.

7. **Advanced Insights and Resources** (Appendix) – Practical tools, checklists, and exercises to keep your skills sharp, including a Glossary of key terms for ease of reference.

Each chapter blends teaching with application. You will find mini case studies, checklists, and access to additional resources throughout the book. Reflection points, mini exercises, and action steps are included throughout each chapter too, to strengthen the learning with practice as we make progress chapter by chapter. My aim is not just for you to understand underwriting in theory but to practice it until it feels natural. Finally, for ease of reference a summary of key terminology is also provided in the Glossary (Appendix Section 2).

Your Journey Ahead

By the time you finish this book, you will no longer look at a deal the same way. You will know how to assess the assumptions, test the numbers, and decide with confidence whether a deal is worth your capital.

More than that, you will see yourself differently. You will not be a passive follower at the mercy of someone else's spreadsheet. You will be an informed, empowered investor with a process you can trust.

That is the transformation waiting for you inside these pages. Let us begin.

P.S. Any additional resources referenced throughout the chapters below, you can also locate at the book resource page here: www.MasteringMultifamilyUnderwriting.com/book-resources.

CHAPTER 1

THE FORECLOSURE EMAIL AND THE DAY EVERYTHING CHANGED

Jane's Ordinary World and Her First Big Deal

The Comfort of Familiar Ground

For years, Jane Morgan considered herself a prudent, measured person when it came to money. She had a respectable career in marketing, a mortgage she could comfortably manage, and a well-balanced portfolio that leaned heavily on index funds. Real estate was something she admired from afar — a market she knew had created fortunes for others, but one she had only dipped into cautiously through a couple of small single-family rentals.

She liked the idea of passive investing. Letting her money work while she focused on her career and family fit her vision of a balanced life. The thought of mailbox money — that alluring phrase tossed around in real estate circles — sparked a quiet ambition. She imagined quarterly checks arriving without fuss or drama, a quiet build toward long-term security.

Her friends often teased her for being "too careful," the one who read the fine print and asked follow-up questions at dinner parties when someone mentioned a "sure thing." Yet, deep down, she was proud of that instinct. It had kept her out of more than one questionable opportunity over the years.

Still, there was a part of Jane that longed to be part of something bigger, something that felt like a step forward into the sophisticated world of high-level investing. And then one day, the opportunity arrived.

The Allure of the Big Deal

It started with a casual conversation at a friend's backyard barbecue. The air was warm, the string lights glowed overhead, and laughter rippled across the yard. Between bites of grilled vegetables, Jane's friend Paul leaned in with an unmistakable sparkle in his eyes.

"You know how you've been wanting to get more into real estate? I think I have something perfect for you," he said.

He explained that he and a few others from their professional network had invested in a multifamily apartment deal in the Sunbelt. The property was in a "fast-growing market" — population up, jobs flooding in. The operator leading the deal was a well-known figure in the real estate circles, the kind of person whose social media posts generated hundreds of comments and whose photo appeared in trade magazines.

"They're projecting a 2x equity multiple in five years," Paul added, as if revealing the punchline to a well-kept secret.

Jane listened closely. She was intrigued, but what really caught her attention was Paul's confidence. He and his wife had already invested, along with several of their mutual friends. He spoke about the operator as though they were a celebrity — charismatic, visionary, and, in Paul's words, "the kind of person who makes deals happen."

Trust by Association

Over the next week, Jane received the glossy investment deck. It was filled with sleek photos of the property — palm trees swaying in the background, sunlit courtyards, and a sparkling pool framed like a resort advertisement. Graphs and charts outlined projected rent growth, expense reductions, and an exit strategy that promised substantial returns.

Jane flipped through each page, nodding along. It all seemed plausible. After all, if many people she respected had already committed capital, was there really much to worry about?

She did what many new investors do in that moment: she equated familiarity with safety. She trusted her friends' judgment. If they believed in the deal — and if the operator had a public persona that radiated success — perhaps this was the leap she had been waiting to take.

She remembered one of the myths she had heard but never challenged: numbers do not lie. The deck's financials looked orderly, professional, and well-presented. Surely that meant the deal was sound.

The Subtle Pull of FOMO

Jane told herself she was making a rational decision, but another force was at play: the fear of missing out.

Her inbox buzzed with updates from the sponsor. Each one carried a sense of urgency — "Limited spots remaining," "Final commitments due by Friday." There was no high-pressure sales pitch, but the subtext was clear: hesitate, and you might lose your seat at the table.

That week, she found herself daydreaming about what this investment could mean. Extra income could accelerate her plans to renovate her kitchen. A solid return might fund more travel, or help her contribute more to her niece's college fund.

She imagined herself five years from now, telling the story of this investment at another barbecue, this time as the one who got in early and reaped the rewards.

The Decision

By Thursday, Jane had made up her mind. She wired $50,000 — a sum she had spent years saving, one that represented discipline, delayed gratification, and countless little sacrifices.

When the confirmation email arrived, she felt a rush of pride. She was finally "in the game." The ordinary world of index funds and slow, steady gains seemed to fade behind her. In its place was the thrill of a new identity: real estate investor.

Foreshadowing Without Warning

What Jane did not know — what she could not know — was that some of the assumptions in that glossy deck were as fragile as glass (more on that later).

These details were invisible to her at the time. She did not yet know how one unrealistic line item in a pro forma could distort the entire picture — or how an operator's reputation could overshadow the rigor of an actual analysis.

A Quiet Shift in Identity

For the moment, all Jane saw was the bright horizon ahead. She had crossed a personal threshold.

At her next family gathering, she casually mentioned her new investment. Her cousin, an accountant, raised his eyebrows. "Multifamily, huh? That's a big move."

Jane smiled. "Yes, but it feels right. I did my research."

In truth, her research had been more about the people's social proof than the property. She had verified the operator's track record through social proof — friends' endorsements, public accolades, and media appearances — but she had not yet developed the ability to independently verify the numbers.

Still, she felt she was on the right path.

The Calm Before the Storm

Life returned to its usual rhythm. Jane poured her focus back into work projects, dinners with friends, and weekend hikes. The investment was set to be a three-to-five-year hold, and the sponsor assured everyone that updates would come quarterly.

Her first quarterly update arrived in her inbox with upbeat language about "steady progress" and "early wins." She did not scrutinize the numbers — the tone alone was reassuring.

In her mind, the deal was unfolding as expected. She had no reason to think otherwise.

A Lesson Waiting to Be Learned

This was Jane's ordinary world at its most comfortable — the stage where confidence came from proximity to others' confidence, where belief in the deal was built on borrowed conviction.

The day would come when that comfort would be replaced by something sharper, something that would change how she approached every investment thereafter.

But for now, she was content. The barbecue conversations, the glossy deck, the shared enthusiasm of her friends — these had carried her over the line. She had stepped into a bigger arena without realizing the rules were far more complex than she had been told.

Her story — and the lessons she was about to learn — was just beginning.

The Call to Adventure — and Sudden Loss

The Email That Changed Everything

Jane was halfway through her first cup of coffee when her inbox pinged. She almost ignored it — mornings were her quiet time before the day's demands took over — but the subject line made her pause:

"Important Update on Your Investment"

It was from the multifamily sponsor she had trusted not too long ago. The one whose reputation in the industry seemed unshakable. The one her friends spoke about with the same tone they might use for a favorite athlete or bestselling author.

She clicked.

> "Dear Investors,
>
> We regret to inform you that the property has gone into foreclosure. Unfortunately, all equity in the project has been lost. We appreciate your trust and are deeply sorry for this outcome…"

The rest of the words blurred.

Her stomach tightened. She reread the email once. Twice. A third time, as if the meaning might change if she looked at it differently. It did not. The $50,000 she had spent years saving was gone. Just like that.

The Shockwave of Loss

Jane's mind raced through the timeline.

She remembered the excitement when her friends told her about the deal. "It is a no-brainer," one had said. "This sponsor has done dozens of deals. I have invested with him three times and made great returns."

She remembered watching the sponsor's webinar, impressed by the polished presentation and slick slides. Rent growth projections seemed strong, the property photos were pristine, and the projected returns — double-digit annualized — felt like a ticket to financial freedom.

The numbers looked professional. The deck was beautiful. The sponsor seemed credible.

So why question it?

She wired the funds without hesitation.

Now, staring at the foreclosure notice, she could not believe how quickly excitement had turned into devastation.

When Trust Replaces Due Diligence

This was not just about the money, though losing $50,000 hurt more than she wanted to admit. It was about what the loss represented — that she had handed over her trust and her capital without truly understanding the deal.

At the time, she thought she was doing her homework. She had read the offering memorandum. She had attended the webinar. She had asked a few questions — though, in hindsight, they were the easy ones, the ones with answers that sounded reassuring.

She had not even considered that numbers can be made to look good while masking fragile foundations — like a house with fresh paint covering rotting beams.

The Blind Spots She Never Saw Coming

The deal, she would later learn, had been built on shaky ground from the start (more on that to come).

The Inner Spiral

In the days that followed, Jane replayed every decision that had brought her here.

Why had she trusted so easily? Why had she taken her friends' endorsement as a substitute for her own due diligence?

A voice inside whispered: *You are not cut out for this.*

Maybe real estate was only for people who had the time to comb through spreadsheets or the expertise to challenge a sponsor's assumptions. She was neither. She was a busy professional, not an underwriter.

The more she thought about it, the more she convinced herself this loss confirmed her worst fears — that she would never be able to protect herself in the world of private real estate investing.

The Hidden Invitation

What Jane could not see yet was that this moment — as gut-wrenching as it was — was her *call to adventure.*

Every hero's journey begins with disruption. Something shakes the status quo, forcing the hero to confront a truth they can no longer ignore.

For Jane, the truth was this:

She could not outsource her judgment.

She could not rely solely on glossy pitch decks, friendly referrals, or the charisma of a sponsor.

If she wanted to keep investing — and she did — she needed to gain the skill to evaluate deals herself.

Foreshadowing the Shift

At this point, Jane did not know that a repeatable, beginner-friendly process for underwriting existed. She did not know that the same principles lenders use to protect their capital could be adapted by individual investors like her.

She only knew that the pain of this loss was not something she wanted to experience again.

She also knew that doing nothing — walking away from real estate entirely — would not bring her closer to her goals.

There was a third path. She just had not found it yet.

If you have ever lost money on an investment, you know how it feels in your body — the heat rising in your chest, the restless nights replaying "what if" scenarios, the hollow frustration of wishing you could turn back time.

Even if you have never experienced it, you might have imagined it. That fear alone can keep many would-be investors on the sidelines.

The question is: what do you do with that fear?

Do you let it stop you from investing altogether?

Or do you channel it into building the knowledge and discipline that can prevent history from repeating itself?

Closing Beat

For Jane, the foreclosure email was both an ending and a beginning.

She had no way of knowing, in that moment of loss, that it would also be the spark that led her to an entirely new way of investing — one rooted in clarity, control, and confidence.

But before that transformation could happen, she would have to face the natural next stage of every hero's journey: the *refusal of the call.*

The doubts. The fears. The pull to retreat.

And that is where we will meet her next.

Reflection Exercise: Think of an investment decision you've made based primarily on someone else's recommendation. What questions do you wish you had asked? Write down three specific concerns you had but did not voice.

Refusal of the Call: Doubt, Fear, and Regret

The Hollow Aftershock

Jane stared at her laptop screen long after the foreclosure email had faded into the inbox below. The polite corporate language of the message could not soften the blow: her $50,000 was gone. She had known losses before — a volatile stock that dipped, a home renovation that cost more than expected — but this was different. This was permanent. There was no "wait for it to recover," no "sell at a better time." It was over.

The room felt smaller. She tried to focus on the hum of the refrigerator in the next room, anything to distract from the sound of her own heartbeat in her ears. Every time she closed her eyes, the words replayed: *We regret to inform you… foreclosure… loss of principal….*

She told herself she was being dramatic. People lost more than this every day. Still, her hands trembled as she clicked away from her inbox.

The truth was more painful than the money itself. She had trusted. She had believed. She had followed the lead of people she thought knew better.

And she had been wrong.

The Inner Jury

That night, sleep would not come. Jane lay awake, interrogating herself like a cross-examining attorney.

Why had she never reviewed the actual numbers? Why had she believed a glossy deck and a polished speaker? Why had she nodded along at a webinar without pausing to ask, *But what happens if the market slows?*

Her own voice turned against her: *You are not cut out for this. You are not an underwriter. You do not even like spreadsheets. You should have known better.*

It was not just the financial loss. The money mattered — of course it did — but what stung was the private shame.

She had told herself she was "doing the smart thing." She had even mentioned it to her family and relatives with quiet pride, framing it as a bold step toward building her financial future. Now she dreaded the conversation that was coming.

Loss in the public eye has sympathy and drama. Private loss just sits with you, tightening your chest every time you remember it.

This was the private cost of investing mistakes that no brochure or seminar talks about — the way it makes you question your own judgment.

The Allure of Retreat

In the weeks that followed, Jane did what many people do when they experience a sudden, embarrassing loss: she pulled back.

She unsubscribed from the investing newsletters she had once opened eagerly. She deleted the podcasts from her phone. When her friends mentioned new opportunities, she smiled politely but changed the subject.

She told herself it was temporary, that she was "just focusing on work right now." But in truth, she had no plan to re-enter the arena. Real estate had felt like a way to build wealth without giving up her time. Now, it felt like a minefield she had no map for.

The voice inside her whispered its verdict again: *Stick to mutual funds. Let the professionals handle it. You are not meant for this world.*

Why the Doubt Feels So Real

Jane's reluctance was not just fear — it was rooted in beliefs she had carried for years.

She believed that underwriting was a specialized skill for "numbers people," not for busy professionals like her. She believed that even if she learned the mechanics, it would be too complex to apply under real-world conditions. And she believed the industry's most dangerous half-truth: *Numbers do not lie.*

But numbers can tell any story the storyteller wants — if you do not know which assumptions to challenge, you will never know whether the picture is accurate or a funhouse mirror.

Jane did not have these words for it yet. She only had the uneasy certainty that she could not trust herself to read the story in the numbers.

The Crossroads of Identity

The loss forced Jane to confront an uncomfortable truth: she had been a follower in her own financial life.

Yes, she worked hard. Yes, she was smart. But when it came to investments, she had outsourced her thinking to other people. She had let the authority of a confident voice, the reassurance of friends, and the excitement of projected returns stand in for her own due diligence.

That realization hurt more than the balance sheet.

If she accepted it, she could either change her role — from follower to informed decision-maker — or she could retreat permanently, telling herself she was "playing it safe" while quietly locking herself out of opportunities.

Right now, retreat felt easier.

When Fear Masquerades as Logic

In conversations with herself, Jane framed her withdrawal as the rational choice:

- She "did not have time" to learn underwriting.

- It was "better to stick to what she knew."

- Real estate was "too risky in the current market."

Reflection Space: It was the same pattern seen in countless other investors after a loss. Fear rarely announces itself directly. Instead, it puts on the clothes of logic and reason.

And without a counterweight — a mentor, a process, a clear path forward — fear can become the quiet architect of a smaller, safer, and ultimately less satisfying financial life.

A Faint Glimmer

One afternoon, weeks after the email, Jane found herself browsing the online portal where her investment statements used to live. She clicked into the "Closed Investments" section and stared at the line item: *Principal Loss — $50,000.*

For the first time, she noticed the tabs she had never clicked before: "Financials," "Market Data," "Operator Notes." All the information she had ignored was there, waiting to be read — perhaps not enough to change the outcome, but enough to make her wonder.

If I had known what to look for, would I have seen the danger?

The question did not yet feel like motivation. But it was the first crack in the wall she had built. Somewhere, under the layers of doubt and regret, a small part of her wanted to know the answer.

And that small part would soon meet the person who could help her find it.

Meeting the Mentor – A New Path Forward

The Coffee Shop Conversation That Changed Everything

Jane sat at the far end of the café, staring into the swirl of foam on her untouched latte. She had been replaying the foreclosure email in her head for weeks. No matter how many times she reread it, the words never softened. Fifty thousand dollars. Gone. Years of saving, the careful budgeting, the overtime hours — erased in a few lines of corporate regret.

Her friends had told her to "shake it off" and that "these things happen in investing." They had already moved on, still attending glossy investor webinars hosted by the same sponsor who had just lost their money (because oh well, he had made them money on other deals…even if it was due to pure luck). Jane could not bring herself to log in. She could not bear the cheerful slides and empty reassurances.

That morning, she was not expecting to meet anyone. But as she scrolled absentmindedly through her phone, a familiar face walked in — a woman she had met briefly at a real estate conference months earlier. Rossi Monroe had been one of the speakers. She was the kind of person who, when on stage, made the room feel smaller. Clear. Calm. No hype, no jargon, just straight talk about deals, risks, and what really happens behind the numbers.

"Mind if I join you?" Rossi asked, setting down a mug of black coffee.

Jane hesitated, but nodded.

Within minutes, the conversation turned to what had happened. Jane admitted she felt foolish. That she should have asked more questions, vetted the deal herself, maybe even passed altogether. But she had trusted her friends' judgment and been dazzled by the sponsor's charisma.

Rossi listened without interrupting.

When Jane finished, Rossi set her coffee down. "You cannot undo the loss, Jane. And beating yourself up for it will not get you anywhere. But you can make sure it never happens again."

Jane's brow furrowed. "How?"

"You learn to underwrite," Rossi said. "Not like a Wall Street analyst, but like an experienced lender and investor — someone who has seen thousands of deals and knows where the numbers hide the truth. You learn to spot the gaps, challenge the assumptions, and see the full picture before you commit a single dollar."

Breaking Through the Limiting Beliefs

Jane leaned back, shaking her head. "I am not an underwriter. I do not have the time to learn something that complex."

"That is what most investors tell themselves," Rossi replied, smiling knowingly. "They think underwriting is a dark art, reserved for analysts in expensive suits. The truth? It is a skill, like learning a language or dancing. At first it feels awkward. You step on your own toes. You get lost in the rhythm. But with the right guide and a clear framework, it becomes second nature."

Jane frowned. "And if I still miss something? Even with training?"

"Numbers can be made to tell any story," Rossi said. "That is why you never stop at the numbers. You look at the assumptions — the rent growth projections, the expense estimates, the reserves, the debt terms. You compare them to reality. You ask: does this make sense in this market, with this operator, at this time? That process is what protects you."

Jane thought about the deal she had lost money on. She remembered how the sponsor had promised aggressive rent growth. She had nodded along, thinking they must know better.

"What if I had challenged those assumptions back then?" she asked quietly.

"You might have passed on the deal," Rossi said. "Or at the very least, you would have still gone in but with eyes wide open."

A Quick Win

Rossi reached into her bag and pulled out a slim folder with a sample pro forma. "Let us do something right now," she said.

"Look here. The broker claims market rents are $1,500. Now, let us check actual comps."

Within minutes, Jane saw the truth. The average was closer to $1,200 — exactly the kind of discrepancy that had burned her before.

She felt a strange mix of anger and relief. Anger that she had once taken such numbers at face value. Relief that, in less than ten minutes, she had spotted the flaw herself.

"That feeling you just had?" Rossi said. "That is the first step toward taking control of your investments. It is not about memorizing formulas. It is about learning where to look, what questions to ask, and when to walk away."

Rossi's Promise

Over the next half hour, Rossi outlined her approach. It was not a jumble of scattered tips or an endless spreadsheet of ratios. It was a simple five-step framework, shaped by years of underwriting both as a lender and as an investor.

"You start with income — rents, other revenue streams, realistic market comps. Then you validate expenses. You check reserves. You evaluate the debt structure. And finally, you analyze the cap rate and the valuation in context with the risks."

Jane took notes as Rossi spoke, her pen flying. For the first time since the foreclosure email, her mind felt clear.

"This is not about becoming a full-time analyst," Rossi continued. "It is about becoming an informed investor who cannot be sold a fantasy. Once you know how to do this, you can look at any deal and decide for yourself — without relying on hype, glossy decks, or someone else's excitement."

Rekindling Confidence

As their cups emptied, Jane realized something had shifted. The tight knot in her stomach had loosened. The fear that had been her constant companion since the loss had started to give way to something else — curiosity.

"What if I really could do this?" she thought. Not as a one-off exercise, but as a repeatable process. She imagined opening a new investment packet, scanning the numbers, and spotting what others missed — both the good and the bad.

She imagined feeling confident enough to tell her friends, "This deal works" or "This one is not worth it" — and knowing exactly why.

"I want to learn," she said finally.

Rossi smiled. "Then you are ready to step across the threshold."

Reflection Space: Every investor will face setbacks. The difference between those who repeat the same mistakes and those who build lasting success is what they do next. Like Jane, you may not be able to erase the past, but you can equip yourself with the tools to shape the future. The moment you decide to take ownership of your analysis — to ask better questions, to dig into the assumptions, to learn the framework — is the moment you reclaim control over your financial destiny.

Crossing the Threshold into Underwriting

The Decision That Changes Everything

Jane stared at the email from Rossi Monroe, her newly found mentor, one more time. The words were simple enough — an invitation to join Rossi's underwriting program — but they felt heavier than anything she had read since that foreclosure notice months ago. It was not the promise of templates or checklists that caught her attention. It was the quiet, unshakable confidence behind Rossi's statement:

> "If you learn to underwrite and vet deals like a professional, you will never again have to invest based on someone else's word."

Jane closed her laptop and leaned back in her chair. She thought about how quickly she had signed on to that ill-fated deal before. The sense of belonging had felt intoxicating. The sponsor's name had been big, the presentation slick, the returns projection dazzling. And yet, here she was — $50,000 lighter, with nothing to show for it.

This was not about getting her money back. It was about making sure the next time she invested, she understood the story behind the numbers. It was about never again feeling blindsided.

She took a deep breath and clicked "Enroll."

The threshold had been crossed.

Stepping Into an Entirely New World

From the moment Jane logged into the program portal, she could feel the difference between the vague confidence of a glossy pitch deck and the grounded clarity Rossi offered. The welcome video opened with a simple sentence:

> "Underwriting is not about memorizing formulas —
> it is about learning to see the truth behind a deal."

Jane liked that. She could handle learning to see.

Still, as she scrolled through the course modules, a flicker of intimidation ran through her. Terms she had only half-heard before — *net operating income, cap rate, yield on cost* — were suddenly everywhere. She remembered how she used to skip over those slides in webinars, assuming they were "just for the analytical types." Now, she could not afford to skip anything.

The first downloadable tool was a market analysis checklist. Jane opened it, expecting something vague and high-level. Instead, it was precise — bullet points on population trends, median household income, job growth, supply-and-demand balance, affordability ratios, and more. This was more than scanning headlines about "hot markets."

Rossi's voice came through in the lesson:

> "The market forms the inputs for your underwriting
> model. If those inputs are wrong, your entire
> analysis will be wrong — even if every formula in
> your spreadsheet is perfect."

Jane underlined that.

The Mindset Shift

As she worked through the first module, Jane realized something unexpected. The biggest hurdle was not the math — it was her own belief that she could not do it.

For years, she had told herself she was "not an underwriter." That was for lenders or full-time real estate pros. She was just an investor who wanted her money to work harder than a savings account. She thought of underwriting the way she thought of reading a legal contract: dense, technical, and meant for specialists.

But Rossi challenged that belief directly:

> "You are not learning this to become a bank. You are learning this to protect your capital. And like any skill — speaking a new language, dancing, playing an instrument — it feels awkward at first. Then, with practice, it becomes second nature."

It was a reframe Jane had not considered. Maybe she did not need to be "an underwriter." Maybe she just needed to become fluent enough to hold her own.

A First Glimpse of the Five Steps

Midway through the welcome module, Rossi introduced the 5-Step Framework that would anchor the program:

1. **Income Analysis and Rent Comps** – Understanding what the property truly earns today and what is realistic tomorrow.

2. **Expense Validation** – Making sure the costs to operate the property are grounded in reality, not wishful thinking.

3. **Reserve Analysis** – Ensuring there is a safety cushion for the unexpected.

4. **Debt Structure and Leverage Considerations** – Choosing financing that supports the business plan rather than strains it.

5. **Cap Rate, Valuation, and Risk Adjustments** – Knowing how pricing and market shifts can impact your returns.

Jane was relieved to see it broken down this way. Five steps felt manageable — not a bottomless pit of spreadsheets.

Facing the First Test

Rossi's first exercise was deceptively simple: look at a real deal summary and highlight any assumptions that seemed overly optimistic.

Jane downloaded the file and started reading. At first glance, the numbers looked fine — annual rent growth of 3%, a two-year renovation plan, reserves set aside for unexpected expenses.

Then she noticed something. The rent comps used for justification were all from Class A properties, yet the subject property was a tired Class B building. Could it really achieve those rents without overspending on upgrades?

She kept going. The reserve line item was three months of expenses — Rossi had just explained that she preferred at least six months. And there was no mention of what would happen if the renovation took longer than expected.

Jane's pen was moving faster now. She had spotted her first red flags.

The Emotional High — and the Reality Check

After submitting her notes, Jane felt a rush of pride. She was starting to see through the "funhouse mirror" Rossi had warned about — the one that could make a deal look attractive from one angle but dangerously distorted from another.

But in the very next video, Rossi brought her back to reality:

> "Spotting issues is step one. Understanding their impact is step two. You can find problems in any deal, but you need to know which ones are deal-breakers and which ones are manageable risks."

That distinction mattered. Jane realized she had spent years conflating the two — either trusting everything or rejecting a deal entirely without knowing why.

The Power of Process

Over the next week, Jane followed the program's rhythm: watch a lesson, apply it to a sample deal, compare her analysis to Rossi's annotated version. Each time, she was surprised by how much she had missed — and how much more she caught the second time.

By day seven, she had a new appreciation for the discipline behind underwriting. It was not about finding the perfect deal. It was about building the muscle to evaluate every deal with the same thoroughness, whether it looked promising or not.

Rossi summed it up in one of their group calls:

> "Good underwriting is not about being pessimistic. It is about knowing exactly what has to go right for the deal to work — and deciding if you believe it will."

Jane wrote that on a sticky note and placed it next to her monitor.

The Threshold Becomes a Path

Crossing the threshold had not been a single moment; it was becoming a series of steps. Every lesson, every exercise, every time Jane spotted a questionable assumption, she was putting more distance between her old self — the investor who followed the crowd — and the new one, who demanded clarity before commitment.

She no longer thought of underwriting as a chore for "numbers people." It was her shield, her compass, and soon, it would be her edge.

As Rossi wrapped up the week's call, she hinted at what was coming next:

> "Most investors lose money not because they cannot run the numbers, but because they trust the wrong ones. In our next session, we will talk about the hidden

risks that burn even experienced investors — and how to avoid them."

Jane closed her laptop, already curious. If there were traps waiting even for seasoned pros, she wanted to know exactly where they were — and how to spot them before they snapped shut.

She was no longer dabbling in the edges of underwriting. She was in it.

And she was not turning back.

Action Step: Identify one investment opportunity you are currently considering. Before proceeding, commit to learning the underwriting process outlined in this book, so you can apply it as you evaluate that deal. Your future self will thank you.

CHAPTER 2

WHY MOST INVESTORS GET BURNED (AND HOW TO AVOID IT)

The Hidden Risks in Multifamily Investing

The First Time Jane Saw the Cracks

Jane was sitting at her kitchen table with a thick, glossy investment deck open on her laptop.

The photos gleamed: freshly painted façades, staged units with granite counters, smiling families in the courtyard. The projected returns sparkled even brighter — double-digit IRR, steady cash flow, a "strong, growing market" just minutes from downtown.

Her friends had already committed. The sponsor, an industry celebrity with thousands of followers, had painted a picture so compelling that Jane felt lucky to have a seat at the table.

She remembered her first mentor session with Rossi Monroe. The seasoned lender-turned-investor had asked her a simple question:

"Jane, what do you think could go wrong with this deal?"

Jane hesitated. "Well… maybe the tenants move out?"

Rossi smiled gently, the way a teacher does before introducing a lesson that will forever change how you see the world.

> "That's one risk. But it is not the only one — and often not even the biggest."

That was the day Jane began to understand that in multifamily investing, the most dangerous risks are the ones you do not see in the brochure.

Why Multifamily Feels Safer Than It Is

For many new investors, multifamily properties carry a halo of safety. The logic sounds airtight: people always need a place to live, apartments are less volatile than single-tenant properties, and with multiple units, vacancy is spread out.

Those statements are not wrong — but they are incomplete.

A multifamily deal can be profitable, steady, and resilient **if** the market is healthy, the underwriting is sound, the operator is capable, the capitalization is adequate, and the financing is structured well.

Miss one of those pillars, and the deal can quickly shift from "solid investment" to "capital loss."

The problem is that the pitch you receive is designed to **highlight strengths** and **downplay weaknesses**. If you do not know where to look, you will not see the cracks until it is too late.

Rossi had spent years on the lending side of the table. She had seen borrowers present flawless pro formas that unraveled within months because the assumptions were misaligned with reality.

She explained it to Jane this way:

> "A pitch deck is like a real estate listing photo. You will not see the broken fence cropped out of the frame. You have to walk the property to see the whole picture."

The Myth That Cost $50,000

Jane recalled her first conversation with Rossi Monroe, as she sat across from her at the small café table, her hands cupped around a mug that had long gone cold. She had just told Rossi about the sponsor who had swept her off her feet — the polished webinars, the raving testimonials, the big promises of "market-beating" returns. She had believed every word.

"What do you think I missed?" Jane asked, her voice low.

Rossi leaned in. "You missed the myths. The stories our industry tells to make the complex seem simple — and the dangerous seem safe. Myths are not always outright lies. They are often half-truths wrapped in a good story. And good stories sell investments."

Jane frowned. "So I was sold a story instead of the truth?"

"You were sold both," Rossi said. "But the story was easier to see. The truth was hidden in the assumptions. Let us look at the myths one by one — so you never fall for them again."

Then she walked Jane through five myths — each paired with a real deal where investors had been blindsided by hidden risks.

Industry Myths and the Cost of Believing Them

Myth #1: "Numbers Do Not Lie"

It is one of the most repeated lines in investing — and one of the most misleading. Rossi explained that numbers are only as honest as the assumptions behind them.

The Rent Growth Mirage: Rossi shared a story where a group of investors was lured into a Tampa property by the promise of $1,700 average rents in an "up-and-coming" neighborhood. The sponsor's model showed steady rent growth, projecting even higher numbers within two years.

On paper, it was a home run.

In reality, market rents were closer to $1,400. A local property manager quietly mentioned that this area had been "up-and-coming" for more than a decade — without ever arriving. Five years later, the rent projections had never materialized. The property underperformed from day one, and the investors never saw their expected returns.

Jane shook her head. "So the numbers were real — but not the truth — overstated rent growth assumptions without credible market validation."

"Exactly," Rossi said. "You must verify the source of every figure. Numbers can tell any story you want them to."

Myth #2: "If the Returns Look Great, the Deal Must Be Great"

Jane admitted that when she had invested before, her eyes went straight to the IRR and cash-on-cash returns. They looked high, so she assumed the deal was strong.

Rossi smiled knowingly. "Many investors do. But I once reviewed a deal that showed excellent long-term returns — except it had no cash flow for the first two years and no reserves. The plan assumed perfect execution in a market with no surprises. That is like planning a road trip with no spare tire, no gas money, and hoping you never hit traffic."

Jane thought about her own deal. "Mine did not cash flow at first either. I guess I thought that was normal."

"It can happen in certain value-add strategies," Rossi said, "but you must ask why. And whether the risk is worth it."

Myth #3: "Cap Rates Always Go Down in Good Markets"

A sponsor in Dallas once marketed a Class B with the assumption that cap rates would compress over time.

"They projected positive rent growth and no stabilization period," Rossi said. "Reserves were three months at best. They were counting on conditions staying perfect. But real estate markets do not work that way."

Jane leaned forward. "So they were betting on a trend instead of preparing for risk?"

"Exactly. Cap rates can go up or down — and sometimes the shift happens faster than anyone expects."

Myth #4: "It's Just About the Deal — the Operator Is Secondary"

Rossi's eyes were steady now. "This one is dangerous. A skilled operator can rescue a flawed deal. A bad operator can sink a solid one."

She told Jane about a heavy value-add deal on a 200+ unit property that looked solid on paper — until the rehab plan revealed zero buffer for delays. The sponsor had layered the capital stack with various fees (above and beyond the norm), even though this was their first heavy rehab deal of such nature. Even worse, the market's rent growth was 0–2%, but the pro forma assumed 3%.

"They did not miss those projections by a little," Rossi said. "They never came close. And because the operator had no margin for error, investors paid the price."

Jane thought about her own deal. "I barely looked at the operator's history. I just assumed my friends had already vetted them."

"That is the trap," Rossi said. "Reputation by association is not the same as proven execution."

Myth #5: "The Market Will Save You"

Jane had once been pitched a deal in a small town "near" a major metro. The sponsor highlighted the proximity but failed to mention that the town's population was shrinking — and it was essentially a single-employer economy.

"When that employer downsized," Rossi said, "occupancy dropped, rents fell, and investors were stuck. The market (and the alleged proximity to the large MSA) did not save them. It accelerated the loss."

Jane nodded slowly. "I guess it is easier to focus on the exciting part of the pitch than the quiet risks."

"That is why you must look for the quiet parts," Rossi said. "They tell you more than the headlines."

The Real Cost of Believing Myths

Rossi pulled out her notebook and drew a quick table — one column labeled "Myth," the other "Cost."

- Numbers do not lie → Paying for a story instead of reality.

- High returns mean a good deal → Taking on hidden risk for the sake of yield.

- Cap rates always go down → Betting your investment on macro trends you cannot control.

- Operator is secondary → Ignoring the single biggest driver of execution risk.

- Market will save you → Underestimating local economic fragility.

"These myths do not just cost money," Rossi said. "They cost confidence. They make you feel powerless — as if you are always one market shift away from disaster."

Jane looked at the list. "So the real skill is not just knowing the numbers — it is knowing what could make them wrong."

Why These Myths and Risks Slip Through

Jane asked Rossi the obvious question: "If these risks are so serious, why would anyone invest without seeing them?"

Rossi nodded knowingly. "Because most investors are looking at the wrong indicators. They are dazzled by projected IRR, cash-on-cash, and equity multiple. They do not pause to ask what assumptions those numbers rest on."

Hidden risks thrive in four blind spots:

1. **Market Misreads** – Assuming growth that is not supported by jobs, wages, or demand.

2. **Operator Overconfidence** – Believing an operator's track record automatically applies to every market and property type.

3. **Financing Fragility** – Using debt terms that do not match the project's timeline or risk profile.

4. **Pro Forma Optimism** – Accepting rosy rent growth, expense reductions, or exit cap rates without stress-testing.

A pro forma is not a crystal ball. It is a narrative. And like any narrative, it can be optimistic, conservative, or somewhere in between. The problem is not the spreadsheet — the problem is relying on it without understanding the assumptions that built it.

Rossi put it to Jane this way:

> "Underwriting is like reading a map through tinted glasses. The roads are real — but the color of the lens

can make some paths look safer or shorter than they are. Your job is to take off the tint and see the true route before you set out."

This realization is what separates the informed investor from the follower. It is not about doubting every deal. It is about verifying every assumption that matters.

Rossi's "Myth-Busting" Checklist

Before they left the café, Rossi gave Jane a mental checklist she still uses today:

1. **Verify, do not assume** — Check every data point with an independent source.

2. **Stress-test projections** — Ask what happens if rents grow slower, expenses rise, or cap rates expand.

3. **Vet the operator as if they were managing your own home** — Track record, experience, and transparency matter as much as the deal itself.

4. **Understand the market's depth** — Look beyond metro headlines to submarket realities.

5. **Look for buffers** — Reserves, time allowances, and conservative assumptions are your insurance.

Jane's Shift

As they walked out into the late afternoon sun, Jane felt something different. The myths that had once wrapped her in a false sense of security now felt like warning signs, she could spot from a mile away.

"I feel like I have been reading a map upside down," she said.

Rossi smiled. "Now you have turned it the right way up. The next step is to stop letting others do your navigating."

Jane had learned the cost of believing industry myths — sometimes measured in lost dollars, but always in lost control. The next step was not just avoiding traps, but stepping into her role as an active decision-maker.

That is where Rossi was leading her next — toward a place where Jane would no longer follow the crowd, but would chart her own course with clarity, confidence, and purpose.

Exercise: Review your last investment decision. Which of these five myths influenced your choice? How would your analysis have changed if you had verified assumptions independently? Create a 'Myth-Busting Questions' list to use on your next deal.

Shifting from Passive Follower to Informed Decision Maker

The Turning Point You Cannot Afford to Miss

For Jane, it began as a quiet, almost unnoticeable shift. She was still the same busy professional juggling work, family, and life. She still loved the idea of passive income and believed in real estate's long-term potential. Yet, after the foreclosure email, the glossy marketing pitches that once lit up her imagination now left her with a faint, uneasy tension. She could no longer hear projected returns without wondering, *what assumptions are hiding behind those numbers?*

This was not cynicism. It was awareness. And awareness is the first step toward transformation.

When Jane first met Rossi Monroe, she still carried the scars of her loss. She was cautious. Skeptical. Unsure if she wanted to invest again at all. Rossi listened, then leaned in.

> "You can be in the passenger seat, hoping the driver knows the road — or you can take the wheel. The choice is yours."

That was the invitation. Not to abandon passive investing, but to abandon *passive thinking*.

Why Passive Follower Mode Is So Dangerous

Many investors, especially when new, fall into what I call "passive follower mode." They believe they are investing passively — which is fine — but what they are actually doing is surrendering their judgment entirely to someone else. It is an easy trap to fall into, and it often begins innocently:

- A friend recommends a sponsor they like.

- A webinar paints an irresistible picture of steady cash flow and appreciation.

- The pro forma looks tidy, the rent growth curve points upward, and the fees are barely noticed.

And so, the decision is made. No market analysis. No verification of assumptions. No understanding of the downside if things do not go as planned.

The industry is full of deals that looked spectacular on paper yet ended in disappointment, as shared in the Myth examples above.

These were not "black swan" events. They were foreseeable risks — risks that could have been spotted by asking the right questions before investing.

The Identity Shift: From Spectator to Strategist

When Jane first began this journey, she saw herself as a spectator in the investing world. She had money to put in, but she believed the "real" experts were the ones running the deals. That belief kept her in the stands, watching the game rather than learning how it was played.

With Rossi's guidance, Jane started to adopt a new identity — one she had not considered before: that of an educated, empowered investor. She was still a passive investor in terms of management, but she was now an *active thinker* in her decision-making.

This shift is critical. Because once you see yourself as a strategist, you stop chasing deals that look exciting and start selecting deals that make sense.

It also changes how you interact with sponsors. You no longer accept vague answers to your questions. You understand the language they use. You spot when rent growth assumptions seem disconnected from market reality, or when reserves are too thin for the risk profile.

And perhaps most importantly, you can walk away — not from investing altogether, but from *that particular deal* — without fear of missing out.

The Skill That Brings Freedom

Many new investors think underwriting is only for sponsors, lenders, or analysts. The truth is that underwriting — even at a basic, sanity-check level — is a form of freedom for passive investors.

It frees you from:

- Blindly trusting others' numbers.

- Feeling pressured by urgency or scarcity tactics.

- Worrying whether you are "missing something" in the fine print.

And it gives you the ability to:

- Evaluate opportunities quickly, even when details are incomplete.

- Focus on deals that meet your personal criteria instead of someone else's.

- Sleep at night knowing you understand both the upside *and* the risk.

For Jane, learning even the first steps of Rossi's framework was liberating. She began with market analysis, understanding that the market sets the stage for all other numbers. Then she moved to the five core elements Rossi insisted every investor should check: income assumptions, expenses, reserves, debt terms, and cap rate projections.

The transformation was not instant. There were moments when spreadsheets felt foreign, when acronyms blurred together, and when she wanted to revert to letting others decide. But each time she pressed forward, she found another layer of clarity.

Dismantling the Excuses

If you are feeling the pull to stay in follower mode, it may be because of one of these beliefs:

"I am not an underwriter."

Neither was Jane. Neither are most investors. Underwriting is a skill, not a birthright. It can be learned step by step.

"It is too complex."

Anything new feels complex at first. Think back to the first time you learned a skill you now use without thinking — driving, cooking, even using your phone. Underwriting follows the same pattern: awkward at first, natural with practice.

"I will still be confused."

Confusion fades with clarity, and clarity comes from doing the work. The more deals you review, the sharper your instincts become.

"Even if I learn it, I could still lose money."

True. No skill eliminates all risk. But the right skill greatly reduces unnecessary risk — and that difference can protect years of your financial progress.

Rossi often reminded Jane that the goal was not to predict the future, but to understand the present well enough to make a rational decision about the future.

Rossi's Advice for the Emerging Decision Maker

Over coffee one afternoon, Jane asked Rossi the question many readers may be asking now:

"How do I know when I have shifted from follower to decision maker?"

Rossi smiled. "When you can explain *why* you are saying yes or no to a deal — without repeating someone else's words — you have made the shift."

It is not about knowing everything. It is about knowing enough to stand on your own judgment.

She offered Jane three guiding principles:

1. **Own Your Criteria** – Decide in advance what returns, risk profile, and market characteristics you will accept. Let the deal meet *your* bar, not the other way around.

2. **Verify Assumptions** – Always trace the numbers back to their source. Ask how they were calculated and what could make them change.

3. **Know the Downside First** – If you understand the worst-case scenario and can live with it, you can invest with a clear mind.

From Fear to Clarity

The biggest change Jane experienced was internal. She began the journey afraid of repeating her loss. By the time she reached this point in her learning, she no longer made decisions from fear. She made them from clarity.

Clarity does not mean certainty. No investor, no matter how skilled, can control all outcomes. But clarity means you understand *why* you are making each decision, what assumptions you are accepting, and where the risks lie.

That shift — from investing with blind hope to investing with informed clarity — is the true hallmark of an empowered investor.

For you this is the point in your journey where awareness becomes your first line of defense. Understanding that hidden risks exist — and knowing they often live in the fine print — will make you far less likely to be blindsided.

For now, I will leave you with Rossi's parting advice from that first lesson:

> "Deals do not fail because of one bad number. They fail because a series of small, unchecked assumptions add up to a big surprise. Your job is to catch them before they catch you."

Your Next Step

As you close this chapter, ask yourself:

- Have I been making investment decisions primarily on someone else's word?

- Do I have my own written investment criteria? For a sample of investment criteria checklist (also covered in detail in the next chapter), go to: www.MasteringMultifamilyUnderwriting.com/book-resources.

- Can I explain the "why" behind my last yes or no?

If your answers leave room for growth, take that as an opportunity, not a judgment. Like Jane, you can make the shift from passive follower to informed decision maker.

In the next chapter, we will strip away the mystery around underwriting itself — what it really is, what it covers, and why understanding it is the foundation for confident, risk-smart investing. You will see that this skill is not reserved for the pros. It is for anyone who values their financial future enough to take the wheel.

CHAPTER 3

MULTIFAMILY UNDERWRITING MADE SIMPLE

What Multifamily Underwriting Really Is

Understanding the Foundation

Before diving into property tours, investment memorandums, or pro formas, every multifamily investor must master one foundational skill: underwriting. It is the backbone of smart investing — the discipline that separates confident, informed decision-making from speculation.

Underwriting is not simply entering numbers into a spreadsheet and hoping the formulas reveal whether to invest. It is a structured evaluation of a property's income potential, expenses, financing, market position, risks, and exit plan to determine if the opportunity aligns with your goals and risk tolerance.

In the simplest terms:

Multifamily underwriting is the process of assessing a property's current and potential performance by analyzing its financials, key

risks, market conditions, and business plan to decide whether it is a sound investment.

Why This Skill Matters

There are four reasons why underwriting is indispensable:

1. **Identifying Red Flags Early** – Financial inconsistencies, unrealistic projections, or market risks surface quickly under careful analysis.

2. **Recognizing Key Risks** – You can assess whether assumptions hold up against market data and operational realities.

3. **Making Data-Driven Decisions** – Choices are based on evidence, not gut instinct or marketing gloss.

4. **Optimizing Returns** – You see where revenue can increase, expenses can be controlled, and value can be maximized.

In multifamily, you are not buying bricks and mortar — you are buying an income stream. Commercial properties are valued based on the income they generate, not comparable home sales. That means your analysis directly influences what you should be willing to pay, the financing you can obtain, and the risks you are taking on.

The 360-Degree View

Strong underwriting looks at the deal from multiple angles, combining what I call the **Five Pillars of Evaluation:**

1. **Market Analysis** – Evaluate the local economy, job growth, rental demand, and demographic trends.

2. **Property Assessment** – Understand the physical condition, unit mix, amenities, and potential for improvements.

3. **Financial Review** – Examine historical income and expenses, rent rolls, and trailing twelve-month (T12) statements.

4. **Debt Structure** – Consider interest rates, amortization schedules, loan terms, and debt service coverage ratio (DSCR).

5. **Exit Strategy** – Determine whether the business plan supports a sale, refinance, long-term hold, or another form of repositioning.

This broad view ensures you are not making decisions on isolated data points. For example, high projected rent growth means little if the local job market is contracting or if the property requires costly, unfunded repairs.

The Art and Science of Underwriting

Underwriting is both an art and a science:

1. **The Science** component represents: the underwriting fundamentals and principals, the hard data, the measurable metrics, and calculations: NOI, DSCR, cap rates, yield on cost, break-even occupancy (these and other key metrics are defined in detail in Chapter 5).

2. **The Art** component represents interpreting assumptions, market trends, and operator capabilities; adjusting for risk; applying judgment to incomplete information through one's own lens of experience and risk tolerance.

For example, science might tell you the property's current NOI supports a certain valuation. The art is in deciding whether projected rent increases are realistic given submarket absorption rates, tenant profiles, or the operator' track record.

The Process in Action

While we will cover the full Five-Step Underwriting Framework in later chapters (Chapter 6), it is useful to understand the logical sequence every underwrite follows:

1. **Gather Inputs** – Rent roll, T12, market reports, lender term sheets.

2. **Verify Assumptions** – Cross-check rent growth, occupancy, expense ratios, and capex timelines with market and property data.

3. **Run the Numbers** – Calculate cash flow, returns, debt metrics, and valuation under base, best, and worst-case scenarios.

4. **Stress-Test the Plan** – Ask: What happens if rent growth stalls? If expenses rise faster than projected?

5. **Decide** – Based on the full picture, determine whether to proceed, negotiate terms, or walk away.

This structure transforms underwriting from a nebulous "spreadsheet exercise" into a clear decision filter.

Key Data Sources and Documents

These are the core documents you will encounter when underwriting a deal:

1. **Rent Roll** – Lists current tenants, lease terms, rents, unit types, occupancy status, and any delinquencies.

2. **Trailing Twelve-Month (T12) Statement** – The property's income and expenses over the past 12 months; reveals trends and anomalies.

3. **Capex Schedule** – Records past capital expenditures and helps gauge future needs.

4. **Tax Bill** – Confirms current property taxes and flags any potential reassessment risk.

5. **Delinquency Report** – Shows late or unpaid rents, which may indicate operational or tenant quality issues.

A disciplined underwriter does not just collect these documents — they scrutinize each for consistency and plausibility.

Common Pitfalls to Avoid

There are five recurring mistakes, *shared Rossi*, that I have observed over the years that stand out:

1. **Neglecting Market Risk** – Focusing on property-level metrics without understanding the surrounding economy.

2. **Missing The Cap Rates** – Assuming future cap rates will contract and not starting off from the right base.

3. **Overly Optimistic Rent Growth or Ignoring Expense Realities** – Assuming future rents that outpace historical or market-supported levels. Using unrealistically low expense ratios to make returns look stronger.

4. **Thin or No Reserves** – Underestimating the buffer needed for unforeseen repairs or market shifts.

5. **Mismatch Between Debt and Business Plan** – Loan terms that do not align with the hold period or stabilization timeline.

Avoiding these mistakes alone can save you from deals that look great on paper but perform poorly in reality.

Why This Is Your Edge

Many investors — even experienced ones — skip or rush their own underwriting because they assume the sponsor's model is sufficient. The danger is that sponsors have incentives to present deals in the best possible light, especially when they are excited about a deal. As a wise person once said: "The beauty is in the eye of the beholder". Your underwriting, when done properly, is your safeguard against bias, error, or overly aggressive projections.

In practical terms, mastering this skill means:

- You can **walk away** from a deal that does not meet your criteria, even if others are rushing in.

- You can **negotiate better** by pointing to concrete findings in your analysis.

- You can **allocate capital confidently**, knowing you have tested the plan under realistic conditions.

Your Next Step

Now that you understand what multifamily underwriting is — and what it is not — the next step is to examine the types of properties you might underwrite. In the following section, we will explore **Asset Classes (A, B, C, and D)**, because the property type you are evaluating will shape every assumption you make and every risk you consider.

The ABCs of Real Estate Investing: A, B, C, and D Property Classes Explained

Why Property Class Matters from Day One

If you have ever read an offering memorandum or sat in a broker's presentation, you have likely heard the terms *Class A*, *Class B*, *Class C*, or even *Class D*. The classification sounds simple, but the implications are deep. Knowing the class of a multifamily property tells you more than its age or curb appeal — it gives you early insight into **expected income stability, operating costs, risk profile, lender appetite, and renovation potential**.

In underwriting, property class is one of the first filters. Before you analyze rent comps, calculate DSCR, or fine-tune your pro forma, you should know exactly what kind of asset you are dealing with. This knowledge sets realistic assumptions for both income and expenses, and prevents you from being swayed by overly optimistic projections.

How Classes Are Determined

There is no universally codified standard for classifying multifamily properties — it is a combination of industry norms, broker shorthand, and lender risk assessment. Still, certain characteristics are widely recognized:

- **Physical characteristics**: Age of the building, quality of construction, architectural style, and condition of common areas.

- **Amenities**: The presence and quality of gyms, pools, clubhouses, parking, and security.

- **Location**: Proximity to jobs, schools, transportation, shopping, and overall neighborhood desirability and safety.

- **Tenant profile**: Average household income, stability, and credit quality.

- **Rent levels**: Relative to market averages.

Let us walk through each class in detail.

Class A (Core) – The Luxury Standard

Class A properties are the most modern and feature-rich apartments in the market. They are typically:

- Built within the last 10–15 years, sometimes even brand new.

- Located in prime neighborhoods with strong job growth and high median household incomes.

- Equipped with premium amenities — resort-style pools, fitness centers, concierge services, high-end finishes.

- At or near the top of the local rent range.

From an underwriting perspective:

Class A properties often have **lower operating expenses as a percentage of effective gross income** (EGI) because they require less immediate maintenance. However, they also have **lower initial yield** — the income return relative to purchase price — because you are paying for quality, location, and stability.

Lender view: These assets may attract competitive financing terms — e.g. lower interest rates — because they are considered lower risk.

Risks to note: In a downturn, Class A tenants may downsize to Class B, creating vacancy risk. Rent growth can be slower if the property is already priced at the top of the market.

Class B (Core Plus) – The Sweet Spot

Class B properties are the workhorses of multifamily investing. They are typically:

- Built 15–30 years ago.

- Located in good, stable neighborhoods — maybe not the most prestigious, but desirable and safe.

- Amenities and finishes are solid but not cutting-edge.

- Rents are slightly below the top of the market, attracting a broad tenant base.

From an underwriting perspective:

Many investors consider Class B the "value-add playground." With targeted renovations — upgraded kitchens, improved amenities, refreshed exteriors — you can push rents closer to Class A levels without the construction risk of developing from scratch.

Operating expenses are higher than Class A but generally manageable. The tenant base is more diverse, often including middle-income earners with stable jobs.

Lender view: Class B assets are still financeable at favorable terms, though lenders may require a bit more DSCR cushion than Class A.

Risks to note: If poorly maintained, Class B properties can drift into Class C territory over time. This "slippage" increases capex requirements and changes the operating profile.

Class C (Value Add) – High Cash Flow, High Touch

Class C properties are older — often 30–50 years or more — and usually located in working-class neighborhoods. They are:

- Functional but dated, with fewer amenities and more deferred maintenance.

- Home to tenants with lower household incomes and higher turnover rates.

- Priced significantly below Class A and B per unit, offering higher cash-on-cash potential.

From an underwriting perspective:

Class C properties can deliver attractive yields, but expenses are materially higher as a percentage of EGI. Maintenance, repairs, and turnover costs require realistic budgeting — lenders and experienced investors often assume **50–60% expense ratios** or higher.

Lender view: Financing can be more conservative — lower LTV, higher interest rates, and stricter underwriting on reserves.

Risks to note: Economic downturns can hit Class C tenants hardest, increasing delinquency and vacancy. The "up-and-coming" story is often used to sell Class C deals, but as the Tampa example from our earlier story shows, not every neighborhood fulfills its promised transformation.

Class D (Opportunistic) – Management Intensive and Risk Prone

Class D properties are the most challenging:

- Often more than 50 years old, with significant deferred maintenance.

- Located in neighborhoods with high crime, low household incomes, and weak economic drivers.

- Minimal or no amenities; tenant base may include those with unstable income or poor credit.

From an underwriting perspective:

Class D deals require **exceptional operational expertise** — experienced property management, robust security, and significant capital for repairs. Expense ratios can exceed 60% of EGI.

Lender view: Financing is limited, often requiring private or hard money sources, and at higher interest rates.

Risks to note: For most new investors, Class D is best avoided. Even seasoned operators take these on only with deep market knowledge and operational resources.

Market Cycle and Asset Class

The different classes behave differently in various stages of the market cycle:

- **Expansion**: Class A thrives as tenants trade up, Class B benefits from spillover demand.

- **Peak**: Class A rent growth slows, Class B and C still see demand from affordability pressures.

- **Recession**: Class A sees tenants move down, Class C can struggle with payment issues, Class B often holds relatively steady.

- **Recovery**: All classes improve, but value-add plays in Class B/C see strong ROI.

Knowing this helps you project rent growth and vacancy in your underwriting model more accurately.

Visualizing Risk vs. Return

Imagine a simple chart:

- On one axis: **Risk** (low to high).

- On the other: **Return Potential** (low to high).

Class A sits at **low risk, lower return**; Class D sits at **high risk, potentially high but volatile return**. Class B and C fall between, each with trade-offs.

This framework is invaluable for deciding if a property matches your investment profile.

Applying This Knowledge in Underwriting

When you begin underwriting, property class should influence:

- **Rent growth assumptions**: A Class A property may have modest growth, Class C may have more potential but also higher risk of stagnation.

- **Expense ratio**: Base expectations on class — e.g., 40% for Class A, 50% or more for Class C.

- **Cap rate expectations**: Class A trades at lower cap rates, Class C/D at higher cap rates.

- **Reserve requirements**: Lenders and prudent investors set higher reserves for lower-class properties.

- **Debt structure**: Class C would require stricter loan terms or more restrictive covenants.

A Quick Cautionary Tale

Rossi Monroe recalls a deal in a "transitional" neighborhood marketed as a Class B repositioning. The building's age and amenities suggested B-, but the tenant profile, crime data, and deferred maintenance told a different story — it was really Class C+. Investors who underwrote it as B-class underestimated turnover costs and overestimated rent growth.

This reinforces the lender mantra: *Always match your underwriting assumptions to the true class of the property, not the one in the pitch deck.*

Practical Exercise: Take three current listings from different submarkets. Based on photos, build year, amenities, and location data, classify each as A, B, C, or D. Then cross-check with broker or sponsor materials. How often do they match your assessment? This exercise builds your ability to see through the marketing spin.

From Knowledge to Criteria

Now that you can confidently identify and classify a property, you have a strong early filter in deal analysis. The next step is to define **what you personally want from an investment** — the balance of cash flow, appreciation, and tax benefits that fits your goals.

That is where we go in the next section.

Investment Criteria: Cash Flow, Appreciation, Tax Benefits

The Three Pillars of Multifamily Returns

When you evaluate a multifamily investment, you are essentially weighing three primary drivers of your returns: **cash flow, appreciation, and tax benefits**. These are the "three pillars" that determine both the character of a deal and how it fits with your personal investment goals.

Many investors overemphasize one pillar — usually appreciation — without realizing how imbalanced their portfolio becomes. In practice, the best outcomes often come from understanding how these pillars interact and deciding ahead of time how much weight you want to give each one.

Pillar One: Cash Flow – The Oxygen of Your Investment

Cash flow is the lifeblood that keeps a property — and your investment — breathing. It is the net income generated after all expenses, debt service, and fees are paid (if capex is not separately reserved for, then it must be factored into the cash flow calculation too…more on that later). Strong, consistent cash flow:

- Covers operating expenses and debt obligations.
- Allows the operator to pay investor distributions.
- Provides resilience during market downturns.

Think of cash flow as oxygen. Without it, even the most promising property can suffocate.

In one of the case studies Jane had reviewed with Rossi, an investor bought into a property that projected significant appreciation but had no positive cash flow in the first two years. When market conditions tightened, there was no safety net. The operator issued a capital call to cover shortfalls — a stressful surprise for passive investors who expected "mailbox money" from day one.

From a practical standpoint, your investment criteria should specify:

1. **Minimum acceptable annual cash-on-cash return** in stabilized years.

2. **Timing of positive cash flow** — does it start immediately or only after a repositioning period?

3. **Reserves coverage** — is there a buffer to maintain operations during lean months?

If you are relying on cash flow for current income, you cannot afford to compromise on this pillar.

Pillar Two: Appreciation – The Growth Engine

Appreciation comes in two forms: **market appreciation** (value increases driven by overall market forces) and **forced appreciation** (value increases from improving the property's net operating income).

Market appreciation can be powerful in high-demand areas — for example, certain California metros have seen double-digit gains over short periods. However, it can also be fickle, tied to broader economic cycles and interest rate shifts. In contrast, forced appreciation through value-add improvements is under the operator's control, though it requires skill, capital, and execution discipline.

The temptation is to chase deals with aggressive appreciation projections. This is where many investors stumble. Recall our Tampa deal example shared earlier. It was marketed as "up-and-coming" with a huge increase in projected rents. Five years later, those rents had barely moved — the appreciation never materialized.

When evaluating appreciation:

1. Look for **evidence** supporting rent and value growth — not just a broker's optimism.

2. Distinguish between **market tailwinds** and **operator-driven improvements**.

3. Consider your **time horizon** — appreciation-heavy deals may have delayed returns, requiring patience and risk tolerance.

Appreciation can be the growth engine, but a car with only a powerful engine and no fuel in the tank is not going far. This is why it must be weighed against your cash flow needs.

Pillar Three: Tax Benefits – The Silent Partner

Tax **deferral** benefits in multifamily investing can significantly improve your after-tax returns, even if they are less visible than cash distributions or value increases. These benefits often include:

- **Depreciation**: The ability to deduct a portion of the property's value each year (a non-cash expense).

- **Cost segregation**: Accelerating depreciation on certain components to front-load depreciation deductions.

- **1031 exchanges**: Deferring capital gains taxes by rolling proceeds into another qualifying property (not very common in multifamily syndications but may be an option if the deal is structured in a way that allows to accommodate 1031 exchanges).

While tax deferral benefits should never be the sole reason for making an investment, they can make a strong deal even better. Think of them as a silent partner who quietly boosts your net returns without demanding attention.

Your criteria should address:

1. Whether the operator is using **cost segregation studies** to accelerate deductions.

2. If the deal structure allows for **1031 exchange participation**.

3. How depreciation allocations will be handled among investors.

4. Last, but certainly not least — note the key word here "deferral" and not "elimination". Depreciation is recaptured at the time of sale. Thus, it is important to work with a real estate savvy CPA who can help you strategically plan and work through potential tax implications or tax strategies specifically tailored for you.

These details matter because they directly influence your after-tax yield.

Weighing the Pillars – Aligning Criteria to Your Goals

Every investor has a different blend that works best for their situation.

These priorities shift based on needs:

- **Cash-flow focused investors** may demand strong, immediate distributions and accept modest appreciation.

- **Growth-focused investors** might tolerate lower short-term cash flow in exchange for higher appreciation potential.

- **Balanced investors** aim for moderate, steady cash flow and appreciation, leveraging tax benefits to enhance overall returns.

Before looking at another offering memorandum, decide:

- What is my minimum acceptable cash flow?

- How much appreciation risk am I comfortable with?

- Do tax benefits meaningfully impact my decision?

This self-defined framework becomes your filter, making it easier to say no to deals that do not fit — no matter how compelling the marketing.

The Danger of Ignoring the Balance

In reviewing hundreds of deals, *Rossi added*, I have seen investors run into trouble when they overweighted a single pillar:

- **Overemphasis on appreciation**: The property from the example noted above, with no early cash flow, collapsed under operating pressure.

- **Overemphasis on cash flow**: Properties in slow-growth markets where income stagnates and exit valuations disappoint.

- **Ignoring tax benefits**: Passing on opportunities where accelerated depreciation could have materially boosted after-tax yield. Or conversely, losing a bid on a deal, because a 1031 exchange investor for whom the tax deferral was of utmost importance decided to overbid on price to win the deal.

Balanced does not mean equal — it means intentional. Your mix should reflect your stage of life, financial objectives, and risk comfort.

A Framework for Applying the Pillars

When a new deal crosses your desk:

1. **Quantify each pillar** — forecasted annual cash flow, projected appreciation (both market and forced), and estimated tax savings.

2. **Stress test assumptions** — lower rent growth, extend vacancy periods, adjust exit cap rates.

3. **Match to your criteria** — if the deal requires conditions that exceed your comfort level in one pillar, it may not be the right fit.

Looking Ahead

How you weigh cash flow, appreciation, and tax benefits will directly affect the type of deals you pursue. In the next section, we will explore how these priorities shift between **value-add** and **stabilized** opportunities — and why getting this distinction right can save you from mismatched expectations.

Understanding Value-Add vs. Stabilized Deals

Why Deal Type Matters Before You Touch the Numbers

One of the fastest ways to derail underwriting is to treat every deal the same. The type of property you are evaluating — whether value-add or stabilized — determines your assumptions, the data you need, your reserve requirements, and the risks you will face. A misclassification can cascade through your analysis, producing projections that look solid on paper but collapse in reality.

Lenders adjust their underwriting models based on deal type. So should you. Understanding this distinction will help you set realistic expectations and avoid the dangerous trap of applying "average" rules of thumb to the wrong kind of deal.

Defining the Two Deal Types

Value-Add

A value-add deal is one where you expect to create meaningful upside in income and/or property value through improvements, operational changes, or both.

Common levers:

- **Renovations:** Upgrading unit interiors, common areas, or building systems.

- **Operational improvements:** Reducing expenses, improving collections, adding revenue streams (e.g., reserved parking, pet rent).

- **Repositioning:** Changing tenant profile, rebranding, or shifting property class.

Key characteristics:

- Current rents are below market potential (but must be proven by actual rent comps, not just broker claims).

- Physical or operational deficiencies that can be corrected with capital investment.

- Potential for measurable NOI growth within a set timeframe.

Stabilized

A stabilized deal is already performing near market potential with minimal need for improvement. It is sometimes called a "core" or "core-plus" investment, depending on age and quality.

Common characteristics:

- High physical and economic occupancy.

- Rents already close to market.

- Minimal deferred maintenance.

- Predictable cash flow from day one.

How Underwriting Changes by Deal Type

1. Income Assumptions

- **Value-Add:** You must model two sets of rents — in-place and post-improvement.

  Example: A $50/unit/month NOI lift from in-place to post-improvement rent for a 20-unit property at a 5% cap rate adds $12,000 per year in NOI and $240,000 in value (= $50/unit x 20 units x 12 months = $12,000 NOI divided by 5% cap rate). But only if the rent lift is realistic, supported by comps, and achieved on schedule.

- **Stabilized:** Focus on verifying that current rents align with market comps. Growth assumptions are modest (often 0% in Year 1, especially in markets where or during periods when rental growth is slowing).

2. Expense Projections

- **Value-Add:** Expect some disruption during renovations — higher turnover, marketing, and maintenance costs. Expenses may spike before they normalize.

- **Stabilized:** Expenses should track historical averages unless you identify inefficiencies. Lenders will often normalize to market and appraisal operating expense (opex) ratios (commonly 45–55% of effective gross income).

3. CapEx Planning

- **Value-Add:** Requires a detailed capital plan, unit-turn pacing, contingency (10–15% is prudent), and soft costs like permits and professional fees. Avoid the heavy-value-add pitfall from the deal example in Chapter 2 that had zero buffer for unit turn delays and a very short timeline for a 200+ unit project... big red flag.

- **Stabilized:** CapEx is mostly for maintenance, not major upgrades. Still include reserves for roof, HVAC, and other large items.

4. Reserves

- **Value-Add:** Larger operating and capital reserves are essential. Six months of expenses is common lender guidance (but setting aside six months of operating expenses AND debt service is more conservative and therefore preferred).

- **Stabilized:** Standard six months of expenses is often a good start if the property is well-managed and the market is stable.

5. Debt Structure

- **Value-Add:** Look for loan terms that align with your business plan. Interest-only periods can improve cash flow during renovations but must match your stabilization schedule. For heavier lift projects, a bridge loan would be the most likely option available.

- **Stabilized:** Fixed-rate, amortizing loans are common; the property's predictable NOI makes it easier to achieve favorable DSCR from day one.

Risk Profiles and Common Pitfalls

Value-Add Risks

- Overestimating rent growth (e.g., our earlier story about the property in an "up-and-coming" area where projected rents never materialized).

- Underestimating CapEx or ignoring soft costs.

- Execution delays — weather, permitting, contractor performance.

- Lease-up taking longer than expected, stretching reserves thin.

Stabilized Risks

- Paying too high a purchase price for predictable income.

- Complacency — assuming stability will last without monitoring market shifts.

- Local economic shifts that impact tenant retention.

When Each Strategy Fits Investor Goals

Goal	Better Fit	Why
Immediate cash flow	Stabilized	Income is already steady; minimal ramp-up.
Long-term appreciation	Value-Add	NOI growth drives forced appreciation.
Tax shelter in early years	Value-Add	Higher depreciation from CapEx and accelerated schedules.
Lower volatility	Stabilized	Fewer moving parts; risk is more about macro factors than execution.

Quick Deal-Type Diagnostic

Ask these yes/no questions to classify the deal quickly:

1. Are in-place rents significantly below proven market comps?

2. Does the business plan require physical improvements or operational changes to hit target returns?

3. Is there a detailed CapEx schedule with unit-turn pacing?

4. Will occupancy or cash flow dip during the hold period to achieve the plan?

5. Are reserves sized for both operating shortfalls and renovations?

If you answer "yes" to most, you are likely in value-add territory.

Practice Calculation

Example: Calculate the value-add impact on the property's valuation.

- Current rent: $1,200/month.

- Post-renovation rent target: $1,250/month.

- Units: 100.

- Cap rate: 5%.

Step 1: $50 rent lift × 100 units = $5,000/month increase.

Step 2: $5,000 × 12 months = $60,000/year additional NOI (assumes no change in expenses).

Step 3: $60,000 ÷ 5% cap rate = $1,200,000 increase in value.

This is the power of value-add — and also why verifying that the $50 lift is realistic is critical.

The value-add strategy also serves as a mitigate against market cycles, but only with proper execution.

As illustrated in the chart below, with steady market conditions (cap rate remains at 5%), improved NOI boosts valuation by 30% ($2.6MM vs. $2MM). Even in a declining market with cap rates rising from 5% to 6%, the same NOI growth preserves value and yields modest 8% property value growth ($2.1MM vs. $2MM).

	Current NOI	Current NOI – Declining Market	Value Add NOI	Value Add NOI – Declining Market
NOI	$100,000	$100,000	$130,000	$130,000
Cap Rate	5%	6%	5%	6%
Value	$2,000,000	$1,666,667	$2,600,000	$2,166,667

Insider Warnings

- Numbers can be made to tell any story. Demand the backup.

- A "light" value-add may have just as much execution risk if the team is inexperienced.

- Stabilized does not mean "set and forget." Market forces still apply.

Your Next Step

Now that you understand how deal type impacts your underwriting, the next step is to gather the **right data** to model each accurately. In the next section of this chapter, you will learn exactly what to pull, where to find it, and how to spot gaps before they become deal-killers.

Key Data Sources and Documents You Must Have

Why Starting with the Right Data Matters

In multifamily underwriting, the accuracy of your analysis depends entirely on the quality of your inputs. If those inputs are incomplete, biased, or outdated, every conclusion you draw will be compromised. This is not a matter of "garbage in, garbage out" — it is "misleading in, money lost out."

Missing or unreliable data is the fastest way to underestimate risk. Even the most sophisticated spreadsheet cannot fix bad inputs. When you know where to find accurate, verifiable information, you reduce your dependence on sponsor-supplied assumptions and can confirm whether the story being told matches reality.

Categories of Essential Data

The sources and documents you need fall into four categories:

1. **Market and Submarket Data** – to assess location strength (we'll cover that in detail in Chapter 4).

2. **Property-Specific Financial Data** – to understand the asset itself and its financial profile.

3. **Legal and Transactional Documents** – to understand the terms, structure, existing contractual obligations, and potential liabilities.

Property-Specific Data Sources

Once the market passes your initial screen, you dig into the property itself.

The non-negotiable property documents are:

- **Rent Roll** – The foundation for income analysis. It usually includes unit types and count, bed/bath counts, occupancy status, lease start/end dates, move-in date, current monthly rents, and any concessions. It is important to confirm that the rent roll rent, when annualized, matches the latest T1-T3 rent trends.

- **T12 (Trailing 12 Months) Income and Expense Statement** – Shows actual financial performance. Beware of "annualized" partial-year statements. This is where you spot trends and gaps in any of the revenue or expense line items. Many lenders would usually take T3 income (as it reflects more recent topline trends) and T12 expenses (some expenses can be seasonal and others one-off; hence why the T3 approach would not apply here; otherwise, expenses would be over- or understated).

- **Unit Mix Summary** – Verify that the number and type of units match the rent roll and physical inspection.

During the preliminary analysis nice-to-have property documents (which should definitely be requested once the property is under contract if they are not already provided) are:

- **Capital Expenditure History** – A record of past renovations and maintenance, which can reveal deferred maintenance risks.

- **Delinquency Report** – Shows the delinquency by unit. Delinquency may be aged too (e.g. 30 days, 60 days, 90 days past due).

- **Trade Out Report** – Useful for spotting the latest lease trends (e.g. are rents for newly leased units going up or down).

- **Tax and Utility Bills** – Useful for validating actual utility expenses of the property and get an idea of how taxes are assessed.

Red Flag: Seeing physical occupancy increase but noticing that the delinquency increases too. This may be an indicator that the owner is filling up units with unqualified tenants.

Legal and Transactional Documents

Even with strong market and property data, the underwriting can fail without operational accuracy.

Detailing these documents is beyond the scope of this guide. However, a list of those documents is available in the complimentary resources of the book (www.MasteringMultifamilyUnderwriting.com/book-resources).

Cross-Verification: The Non-Negotiable Habit

During her underwriting workshops with Rossi, one of the most impactful habits Jane learned is **cross-verification** — using at least two independent sources for every key data point.

For example:

- Verify rent comps through both CoStar and your own mystery shopping calls.

- Compare crime stats from the police department with real estate investor forums or property manager feedback.

- Validate T12 expense adjustments against lender underwriting guidelines.

This step is not about distrust — it is about discipline.

Jane breathed a sigh of relief: "Once I know exactly which data sources and documents I must have, I can remove a huge source of uncertainty from the underwriting process."

"Exactly," said Rossi. This is your foundation — without it, every assumption is guesswork. With it, you are no longer at the mercy of glossy marketing materials or over-optimistic projections. You can stand in front of any deal, ask the right questions, and make decisions from a position of strength.

Now that you understand what multifamily underwriting encompasses and can classify properties confidently, we need to address the foundation that determines whether any property can succeed: the market itself. Because as you'll learn in Chapter 4, even the best property analysis is worthless if the market cannot support your business plan. No matter how strong a property looks on paper, the wrong market can turn a promising deal into a costly lesson.

CHAPTER 4

MARKET AND SUB-MARKET ANALYSIS

Why Market Selection Is the First Filter

The Costliest Shortcut You Can Take

As Rossi and Jane continued their journey together, Rossi recalled the following story.

The email subject line read: *"You won't believe this off-market deal—act now!"*

It came from a respected syndicator with a reputation for sourcing hidden gems. The photos looked promising. The numbers? Even better. High projected cash flow, double-digit IRR, and a debt structure that looked like it had been blessed by the real estate gods.

The investor who received that email—let us call her Melissa—did what many eager investors do. She dove straight into the pro forma, ran every ratio, and imagined the property anchoring her portfolio. Weeks later, she made the trip to see it in person.

The neighborhood told a different story. Vacant storefronts, grass sprouting through cracked sidewalks, a police cruiser idling on the corner. Her property manager, who had quietly toured the area ahead of her, shook his head: *"You'll be fighting delinquency from day one."*

Melissa's hours of spreadsheet work had been wasted, not because she miscalculated the NOI, but because she skipped the very first—and most important—step: making sure the market could carry her investment.

Why Market Comes Before the Math

One of the first things I tell new investors, *Rossi added*, is this: *If you start your underwriting with the deal, you are already behind.*

Before a single rent roll is reviewed or a single expense line is questioned, the market needs to pass your criteria. This is not just a matter of "location, location, location" as the old saying goes—it is about understanding the **underlying forces** that will either protect or erode your investment over time.

From the training room to the field, I have seen how often people reverse the order. They start with a deal they like emotionally, then go looking for reasons to justify it. This is backwards. The market is the filter. If the filter is clogged, nothing good gets through, no matter how polished the property looks.

A strong market is not just a setting—it is a *tailwind*. It pushes occupancy higher, supports rent growth, and helps you ride out downturns. In contrast, a weak or declining market acts like an anchor. Even the best operator, the smartest renovation plan, and the most favorable financing can be dragged down by the wrong location.

Seeing Market as a Protective Tailwind

Imagine two identical properties. Same vintage, same condition, same renovation plan. One sits in a city with steady population growth, a diversified job base, and strong rent demand. The other sits in a city where the largest employer just announced layoffs, vacancy rates are creeping up, and people are moving away.

On paper, you might be able to make the weaker-market property look appealing—especially if the price per unit is lower. But the "discount" is an illusion. The moment the market softens, the weaker location will lose tenants faster, take longer to re-lease units, and force you to make rent concessions you never budgeted for. Your projected returns vanish, not because you mismanaged the asset, but because the market was not working in your favor.

By contrast, the strong-market property has a built-in safety net. Even in a downturn, in-migration and job stability keep demand healthy. You may have to slow rent increases, but you are far less likely to slash rents just to maintain occupancy. Over a hold period, that tailwind can be the difference between surviving a rough patch and losing the asset.

The One-Employer Town

Years ago, *Rossi recalled*, I reviewed a deal in a small Midwestern town. The numbers were textbook perfect—low acquisition price, solid cap rate, and attractive cash-on-cash. But something in my gut told me to check the employment base.

It turned out that 40% of the town's jobs came from a single manufacturing plant. The next largest employer was the school district. Six months after I passed on the deal, the plant announced it was relocating overseas. Within a year, vacancy in the local rental stock doubled, property values cratered, and several apartment owners I knew were in workout negotiations with their lenders.

The lesson? Market risk is not always visible in a broker's offering memorandum or the syndicator's pitch deck. You have to look beyond the deal into the ecosystem that sustains it.

Why Investors Skip This Step

"If market selection is so important, why do so many investors gloss over it?" Jane asked. "There are a few common reasons," Rossi added:

- **Excitement Bias** – A "hot" deal creates urgency that overrides due diligence discipline.

- **Data Overload** – Market research can feel messy compared to the tidy structure of a pro forma.

- **Overconfidence in the Operator** – Trusting a well-known sponsor can lead investors to assume the market has already been vetted.

- **Misplaced Frugality** – Skipping thorough market research to save time or money is like refusing a home inspection before buying a house.

These shortcuts may save a few hours upfront, but they can cost years of lost returns—or the entire investment.

The Tailwind in Practice

The "tailwind" analogy is not just poetic—it is rooted in real dynamics. When you invest in a growing market:

- **Rising Population** → Expands your tenant base over time.

- **Healthy Job Growth** → Increases tenants' ability to pay and absorb rent increases.

- **Diverse Economy** → Reduces exposure to the failure of any single industry.

- **Constrained Supply** → Keeps vacancy low, even when demand cools.

These factors give you margin for error. If your renovation runs long, the market may still lift your occupancy. If interest rates rise mid-hold, appreciation from rent growth can help offset financing pressure. In other words, the market can help correct small mistakes—or at least soften their impact.

By contrast, in a flat or declining market, even flawless execution may only produce mediocre returns. You are rowing against the current.

Your Current Portfolio's Tailwind

Take a moment to look at any investment you currently hold or are considering.

Ask yourself:

1. If the broader economy slowed tomorrow, would this market still attract new residents?

2. If a major employer closed, how quickly could the market replace those jobs?

3. Has this market's population and income been rising, flat, or declining over the last decade?

If your answers are uncertain or negative, you may be relying on the property itself to fight headwinds the market is creating. That is not a battle you want to fight.

Lead with the Market

Rossi further shared with Jane: "The most sophisticated investors I know—family offices, institutional buyers, seasoned syndicators—never start with the deal. After vetting the operator, they start with the market.

They know that a market with strong fundamentals makes every other aspect of the investment easier, from leasing to financing to eventual sale. They also know that when the cycle turns, the right market can be the life raft that keeps their portfolio afloat."

As we move into the next chapters, we will break down exactly what "strong fundamentals" look like and how to measure them. But before we do, commit to this simple rule:

No market, no deal.

Because the best way to win in multifamily is to have the wind at your back before you ever take the first stroke.

Key Market Metrics to Watch

The Right Numbers Tell the Right Story

Rossi leaned over Jane's laptop as spreadsheets filled the screen.

"Numbers do not lie," she said, "but they can mislead you—especially if you start with the wrong ones."

Jane frowned. "I thought underwriting was all about the property's income and expenses."

"It is," Rossi replied, "but those numbers are shaped by forces much bigger than the property itself. The market sets the stage. And the only way to know if that stage can support your performance is to look at the right market metrics—before you get emotionally attached to a deal."

From Philosophy to Practice

In the last section, we discussed why market selection is your first filter—your protective tailwind. Now we turn to the practical side: the specific metrics that tell you whether that tailwind is working for you or against you.

Think of these as your **market health indicators**. They are not random statistics. They are the numbers that:

- Predict demand for rental housing.

- Signal stability or vulnerability in local economies.

- Warn you when affordability might cap rent growth.

- Reveal whether supply is working in your favor or flooding the market.

Each metric gives you part of the picture. Together, they let you make an informed, confident decision about whether to proceed—or pass—before diving into property-level underwriting. And most importantly, these metrics provide the inputs (assumptions) for the outputs (proforma cash flow and returns that we will dive into in Chapter 6).

The Core Market Metrics

Population Growth

Why it matters:

Population growth drives household formation and therefore housing demand. More people means more *potential* renters, which supports occupancy and rent growth over time.

Population growth does not automatically mean rental demand. Household formation is what drives the demand and it is an important factor to consider.

Rule of Thumb:

- At least **1% annual growth** for large markets (500K+ population).

- Faster growth for smaller cities (as the population base is smaller).

- At a minimum, outpacing the U.S. national average is ideal.

Where to Find It:

- **Free Sources:** U.S. Census Bureau, City-Data, and Department of Numbers.

- **Paid Tools:** CoStar and Yardi Matrix.

Example:

Rossi had Jane compare two cities: Orlando, FL (2%+ population growth for several years) and St. Louis, MO (flat to declining). "In Orlando," Rossi explained, "you could make a few mistakes in execution and the market's momentum might still carry you. In St. Louis, you have to be flawless just to maintain your baseline."

Job Growth and Employment Trends

Why it matters:

Jobs bring people. People pay rent. Strong job growth signals a healthy local economy (which also makes it attractive for people to move to that market) and the ability for residents to absorb rent increases.

Rule of Thumb:

- **2%+ job growth** year-over-year or at least above the national average.

- Low unemployment (at or below the national rate).

- Pay attention to *net job growth*, not just percentage increases.

Where to Find It:

- **Free Sources:** Bureau of Labor Statistics (BLS), local economic development agencies, DepartmentOfNumbers, and DataUSA.io.

- **Paid Tools:** Brightinvestor.com, RealPage, Yardi, and CoStar analytics.

Median Household Income and Affordability

Why it matters:

A tenant's income determines whether they can pay rent now—and after increases. Low income relative to rent can lead to higher delinquency and turnover.

Rule of Thumb:

- **Median Household (HH) income of $50K+** (this number would vary by market and your target tenant base; it will also adjust over time with inflation).

- **Rent-to-income ratio** ideally 25% or less but no more than 30% (which effectively means that rent expenses represent 30% of the income for that person, i.e., if higher than that, it may create affordability constraints).

- **Growth in income** should keep pace with or exceed rent growth ideally.

Where to Find It:

- **Free Sources:** Census QuickFacts, Department of Numbers, and CensusReporter.

- **Paid Tools:** Brightinvestor, RealPage, and Yardi.

Example:

In a submarket Jane evaluated, median household income was $45K, and the average two-bedroom rent of $1,125 consumed 30% of that. Rossi pointed out that any significant rent hike would quickly push the market into affordability stress—a recipe for concessions, delinquencies, and tenant churn.

Job Diversity

Why it matters:

A city relying heavily on one employer or industry can collapse if that employer leaves or that industry suffers.

Rule of Thumb:

- No single employer should represent more than 15% of total employment.

- Mix of industries including recession-resistant sectors (healthcare, education, government) and export related industries (manufacturing, trade, service providers, etc.).

Where to Find It:

- **Free Sources:** Local Chamber of Commerce, economic development reports, and DataUSA.io.

- **Paid Tools:** Brightinvestor.

Example:

Jane once reviewed a property in a market showing 3% job growth. She was excited until... Rossi showed her that 70%

of those "new" jobs were in a single fulfillment center. "That is not job diversity," Rossi warned. "It is a concentration risk dressed as growth."

Crime Trends

Why it matters:

High or rising crime discourages residents, drives up turnover, and depresses property values. Even a great property will struggle if tenants do not feel safe.

Rule of Thumb:

- Crime index below the US national average (or under 500 for City-Data) and declining year over year.

- Violent crime rates low to none and generally declining year-over-year.

Where to Find It:

- **Free Sources:** SpotCrime, NeighborhoodScout, JusticeMaps, and City-Data.

- **Boots on the Ground:** Property managers and local investors.

Example:

Jane once looked at a property in a "hot" metro. On paper, everything looked fine. But SpotCrime maps showed a cluster of assaults and robberies within a few blocks. Rossi asked: "Would you walk here at night? If the answer is no, your tenants will feel the same."

Rent Growth

Why it matters:

Consistent, moderate rent growth signals healthy demand. Extreme spikes are often unsustainable unless backed by wage growth and influx of net in-migration.

Rule of Thumb:

- Historical rent growth of 2%–3% annually is sustainable (i.e., it aligns with the rate of inflation), but it varies by market. And during periods of market downcycle, rent growth can quickly turn negative.

- Match rent growth expectations to local wage trends and the long-term historical average for that specific market.

- Consider **demand and supply dynamics**, as an influx of supply will dampen rent growth over time (and can actually lead to rent decline).

Where to Find It:

- **Free Sources:** ApartmentList, Zumper, Rentometer, and HUD data.

- **Paid Tools:** CoStar, Real Page and Yardi Matrix.

Example:

Certain Sunbelt markets saw unsustainable double-digit rent growth in the early 2020s — a reminder to always check the long-term trend. Rossi warned Jane: "Do not underwrite as if that pace will continue. Look at the 5–10 year trend."

Median Home Values & Rent-to-Own Ratios

Why it matters:

High home prices relative to rents make renting more attractive. Low home prices can draw renters into ownership, reducing your pool.

Rule of Thumb:

- Rent-to-own ratio over 50% suggests a strong renter base.

- Steady home price growth supports property appreciation.

Where to Find It:

- **Free Sources:** U.S. Census, Bestplaces.net, City-data, and DataUSA.io.

- **Paid Tools:** CoreLogic and CoStar.

Example:

Jane compared two submarkets. In one, monthly mortgage payments were $900; in the other, $1,800. "Which one will keep people renting longer?" Rossi asked. Jane smiled—the answer was obvious.

Supply, Demand, and Absorption

Why it matters:

Too much new supply without matching demand can drive up vacancy and force rent concessions.

Rule of Thumb:

- Positive and increasing absorption (more units rented than delivered) is a good sign.

- New supply growth under 2% of inventory is generally ok.

Where to Find It:

- **Free Sources:** Local planning department, broker reports, etc..

- **Paid Tools:** CoStar pipeline data and Yardi construction reports.

Example:

A market Jane studied had strong job growth but 6% of its inventory was under construction with another 1,000 units in the pipeline. Rossi cautioned: "Even good markets can be overbuilt."

Quick Reference – Market Metric Ranges

Metric	Ideal Threshold
Population Growth	1%+ annually
Job Growth	2%+ annually
Median HH Income	$50K+
Rent-to-Income Ratio	≤ 25%
Crime Index	< 500, declining

Rent Growth	2%–4%
Rent-to-Own Ratio	> 50%
Supply Growth	< 2% of inventory
Job Diversity	No single employer > 15%

Exercise – Your Market's Health Check

Pick one market you are interested in.

1. Find its population growth rate over the past 5 years.

2. Identify its top 5 employers and industries.

3. Check its median household income and rent-to-income ratio.

Ask yourself: *Would this market provide a tailwind for my investment—or an anchor?*

Numbers Before Narrative

Rossi summed it up for Jane: "These numbers are not trivia. They are your early warning system. Get them right, and you can underwrite with confidence. Get them wrong, and you are building on sand."

Strong underwriting starts with knowing the market can support your business plan. When you understand these metrics, you are no longer guessing—you are making strategic, informed decisions that protect your capital and position you for growth.

Passing the market-level test is not enough; the next step is the neighborhood filter.

You can find the complete market analysis checklist at: www. MasteringMultifamilyUnderwriting.com/book-resources.

Submarket Deep Dive: Neighborhood-Level Insights

Two Properties, Two Worlds

Jane was surprised.

On paper, the two properties looked nearly identical—built in the 1980s, similar unit counts, both in Orlando, Florida. The pro formas showed nearly the same projected returns.

But when Rossi pulled up a map and layered in crime data, school ratings, and income statistics, the similarities vanished. One sat in a neighborhood with steady income growth, low crime, and proximity to major employers. The other was in a pocket with violent crime rates twice the city average, declining household income, and boarded-up retail just blocks away (aka Parramore…though you could not have told that solely by looking at the broker's package and the pictures).

Rossi's verdict was quick: "One of these is a safe bet for long-term stability. The other will keep you up at night. Same city, completely different risk profile."

Why Submarkets Matter

Passing the *market* filter is only the first victory. Inside every strong city are neighborhoods—submarkets—that can make or break your investment.

A city may show great population and job growth on a macro level, but if the property sits in a pocket of high crime, weak demographics, or economic decline, your returns will suffer.

Submarket analysis is about zooming in until you understand the property's immediate operating environment. In some cities, the landscape could change from one block to the next. This is where you assess whether your tenants will want to live there, stay there, and be able to pay rent over time.

The Five Major Risk Signals

From years of reviewing deals, *Rossi shared*, these are the neighborhood-level red flags that should trigger deeper review—or an immediate pass.

1. Crime Rate and Type

Crime statistics are one of the clearest indicators of neighborhood risk. While some level of crime is inevitable in urban areas, *violent crime*—shootings, assaults, robberies— directly impacts resident safety and retention.

What to Look For:

- Crime index below the US national average and trending downward.

- No or minimal and declining violent crime rates year-over-year.

- Avoid areas with concentrated clusters of incidents within walking distance of the property.

Tools & Sources:

SpotCrime, NeighborhoodScout, local police crime maps, property manager feedback.

Example:

Rossi shared a story with Jane: "I once came across a deal that someone had brought to me for a second set of eyes review. The numbers looked ok until...I looked up the market — multiple shootings within 1 mile of the property, low median household income...you get the picture. Needless to state, the investor passed on the deal and was appreciative of me pointing it out.

"Another example, Rossi added, was with another property looking great on paper...until we looked up the area — declining population, low median household income, definitely more of a Class C-...all of which made the rent growth and appreciation assumptions a pie in the sky."

2. Property Condition and Pride of Ownership

A drive-through of the surrounding streets can reveal a lot: landscaping, road maintenance, paint condition, and the presence (or absence) of deferred maintenance.

Why It Matters:

Poor upkeep often correlates with low income, high crime, or disengaged landlords—all of which make it harder to raise rents and retain good tenants.

Tip:

If the city is not maintaining roads or public spaces, it may also be slow to provide the services your tenants rely on.

3. Vacancy and Population Decline

Visible vacancies—boarded windows, empty retail, low vehicle counts—are red flags. High vacancy often stems from deeper problems: job loss, crime, or an exodus of residents.

Why It Matters:

High vacancy forces owners to compete harder for tenants, often leading to rent concessions and weaker collections.

Data Sources:

Google Maps, walking the area during the day and night, local boots on the ground trusted contacts.

Example:

Rossi shared: "I once reviewed a deal in a declining population market sold as being "close to a large MSA." The submarket itself had lost residents for years, and the "proximity" did not help fill units when the nearest major employers were a 45-minute drive away."

4. Weak Demographics

Even if the citywide median household income looks healthy, the specific neighborhood could tell a different story.

Key Indicators:

- Poverty rate over 15–20%.

- Median household income below $50,000.

- Unemployment rate more than 2% above the city average.

These conditions directly affect delinquency rates, the ability to raise rents, and overall property stability.

5. After-Dark Reality Check

Data and maps are essential, but there is no substitute for visiting the property at different times of day—especially after dark.

What to Look For:

- Peaceful, quiet streets vs. large groups loitering, loud disturbances, visible drug activity.

- Comfort level—would you walk here at night? Would your property manager take on this building?

Rossi's rule: "If you would not live here, be careful about buying here."

Positive Signals and the "Path of Progress"

Not every rough-looking neighborhood is off-limits. Some are in the early stages of revitalization. The "path of progress" refers to areas adjacent to stronger neighborhoods where public and private investment is already underway.

Positive Signs Include:

- Announced infrastructure projects (new transit lines, road upgrades).

- New retail or mixed-use developments.

- Rising home values and incomes outpacing surrounding areas.

- Public plans for rezoning or redevelopment.

Caution:

Speculating on future improvement is risky. The change must be real, measurable, and already in motion—not just a hope.

Data + Boots on the Ground

Step 1 – Online Research

- Crime maps, census data, rent comparables, property sales history.

- Google Street View for visual condition checks.

Step 2 – Local Intelligence

- Property managers: "Would you manage here? At what rent level?"

- Brokers: "What class of tenants do you see moving in and out?"

- Other owners/investors: "What is your collection rate in this area?"

Step 3 – Site Visit

- Drive the streets within a 1-mile radius.

- Visit at multiple times of the day.

- Walk the property perimeter and nearby amenities.

Exercise – Your Submarket Reality Check

Pick a property address you are interested in.

1. Pull crime data for a 1-mile radius from Spotcrime. com.

2. Identify median household income and poverty rates for the census tract.

3. Check Google Street View for property condition and neighborhood upkeep.

4. Call a local property manager (or a boots on the ground contact you have) and ask if they would manage (live) there.

Write down: *Would this submarket support my business plan—or fight against it?*

The Second Filter

Strong cities can hide weak neighborhoods. Submarket analysis is your second filter—your chance to catch risks that the market-level view misses.

Rossi's advice to Jane applies to every investor:"Passing the market test is good. Passing the submarket test is essential. You are not buying the city—you are buying this block, this street, this property's reality. Make sure it is one you can win in."

To obtain a copy of the complete sub-market analysis checklist, go to: www.MasteringMultifamilyUnderwriting. com/book-resources.

How to Weigh Market Risks Against Potential Returns

The Temptation of Bigger Numbers

Rossi slid two deal summaries across the table to Jane.

The first: a 92-unit property in a growing, diversified market. Steady rent growth, low crime, healthy job diversity. Projected IRR: **14%**.

The second: a 108-unit property in a market with population decline, one major employer, and a spike in crime over the last three years. Projected IRR: **20%**.

Jane's eyes went wide. "That is a six-point difference. How can we pass on that?"

Rossi smiled. "Because in this business, bigger numbers often mean bigger risks. The question is not *what you might make*—it is *what you might lose* and how quickly."

Why Higher Returns Often Signal Higher Risk

Deals in weaker markets often advertise higher projected returns to attract investors. That is not always a bad thing—but you need to ask *why* those returns are higher.

Sometimes, it is because acquisition prices are lower. Sometimes, because the pro forma assumes aggressive rent increases or unrealistically low vacancy. And sometimes, it is because the market fundamentals are so shaky that operators must dangle bigger carrots to get anyone interested.

Common red flags behind "too good to be true" numbers:

- Flat or negative population growth.
- Overreliance on a single industry or employer.
- Crime rates trending upward.
- New supply flooding the market.
- Operator using rent growth assumptions that outpace wage growth.

The headline return may look appealing, but if the underlying market is fighting against you, those numbers will not hold when reality sets in.

The Risk/Reward Equation

The core question: **Do the potential rewards justify the market risk?**

Here is a simple framework Rossi taught Jane to use:

1. **Market Strength** – Rate the market's fundamentals (population, jobs, incomes, diversity, crime) on a scale from 1 to 10.

2. **Risk Factors** – Identify specific vulnerabilities (single employer, overbuilding, affordability pressure, crime trends).

3. **Projected Returns** – Look at IRR, cash-on-cash, equity multiple.

4. **Probability of Achieving Returns** – Based on the market's stability, how likely is the pro forma to hold?

5. **Downside Scenario** – What happens to your returns if rent growth stalls, vacancy rises, or expenses increase faster than expected?

Example:

- Deal A: Strong market (score: 9/10), IRR 14%, low downside risk.

- Deal B: Weak market (score: 4/10), IRR 20%, high downside risk.

Which would you choose? Jane learned that smart investors often take the lower return if the risk-adjusted yield is actually higher.

Stress Testing the Deal

Rossi made Jane run both deals through a stress test:

- Reduce rent growth to **0% in year one, 1% thereafter**.

- Increase vacancy by **3% above pro forma**.

- Increase expenses by **5%**.

- Expand exit cap rate by **50 bps more** than underwritten.

Result:

- Deal A still produced an 11% IRR.

- Deal B dropped from 20% to 5%—and barely covered debt service in two of the hold years.

"That," Rossi said, "is why you do not chase numbers without understanding the market risk behind them."

Case Examples

Case 1 – The Illusion of Cash Flow

A 150-unit property in a stagnant Midwest city promised an 18% IRR. The first year looked fine. By year two, a major employer left. Vacancy climbed to 25%, rent concessions wiped out NOI, and the sponsor issued a capital call just to keep the lights on. Investors who bought into the "great numbers" story ended up with a negative return.

Case 2 – Risk with Mitigation

A 72-unit deal in a higher-crime area of a Sunbelt city projected a 19% IRR. The difference? The operator had already secured a major nearby employer as a long-term corporate housing partner, locking in 40% of the property's occupancy at premium rents. The market risk was still there, but it was offset by a contractual revenue stream.

Case 3 – The Safe Play That Won Long-Term

A Class B property in a strong Texas metro projected a modest 13% IRR. The market's tailwinds carried occupancy above projections even during a national downturn. When sold, the property outperformed the original IRR by three points—without the sleepless nights that come with higher-risk markets.

Investor Personality & Risk Appetite

Not every investor has the same comfort level. Some will take calculated risks in a thin market if the upside is compelling and they trust the sponsor's plan. Others prefer steady, predictable markets even if returns are smaller.

Rossi's guidance to Jane: *"Know your personal risk profile before you look at another deal. Decide your comfort zone for market risk so you can pass quickly on anything outside it."*

Ask yourself:

- Am I comfortable with the possibility of a capital call?
- Would I accept break-even cash flow in exchange for a chance at a bigger back-end payout?
- Do I value steady income more than a large speculative gain?

Your Own Risk/Return Test

Pick a deal you are evaluating (or one from a past offering).

1. Score the market's fundamentals from 1–10.

2. List the key risk factors.

3. Run a stress test: lower rent growth, raise vacancy, and increase expenses.

4. Compare the "base case" vs. "stress case" returns.

Would you still invest if the stress case came true? If the answer is no, you may be looking at a return mirage.

Keeping the Return You Earn

It is easy to be seduced by a glossy offering promising outsized returns. The discipline comes in asking: *What is the market risk behind this number, and can I live with it?*

As Rossi reminded Jane, "It is not about chasing the highest return—it is about keeping the return you earn."

When you evaluate market risk with the same rigor as the property's financials, you protect your capital, your peace of mind, and your ability to stay in the game long enough to win.

By now, you can see why the market and submarket are the filters every deal must pass before you even touch the numbers. In the next chapter, Rossi shifts Jane's focus to the property's financials themselves — but first, she makes sure Jane understands the key terms and concepts that form the language of underwriting. Without this foundation, even the best spreadsheet becomes a guessing game.

With market fundamentals as your foundation, you are ready to dive into the property's financial engine. But before we do that, in Chapter 5, we'll dive into understanding key terminology and key performance indicators that will later on, in Chapter 6, arm us with the necessary language and help us examine how to perform financial analysis on a property — the building block that determines whether those market opportunities translate into actual returns.

CHAPTER 5

KEY TERMINOLOGY AND CORE CONCEPTS

Income Metrics: Gross Potential Rent, Loss to Lease, and Effective Rent

The Hidden Truth Behind "Top-Line" Numbers

Jane squinted at the neatly formatted deal summary Rossi had slid across the café table.

"Look at that," Jane said, tapping the first line. "Gross Potential Rent (GPR) — over two million. This property must be a home run."

Rossi smiled, the kind of smile that says *you are about to learn something important.*

"That," she said, "is the illusion that trips up more investors than you think. GPR is a starting point, not the finish line. Without knowing what is hiding beneath it, you might as well be judging a book by its dust jacket."

Why These Three Metrics Matter First

In multifamily underwriting, your income assumptions are the foundation of the entire deal model.

If those assumptions are inflated or poorly understood, every downstream metric — from Net Operating Income (NOI) to projected returns — becomes unreliable.

Three terms form the top of the income stack are:

1. **Gross Potential Rent (GPR)**
2. **Loss to Lease (LTL)**
3. **Effective Rent**

Understanding these terms is not simply about memorizing definitions. It is about grasping how they interact, how they are calculated, and how they can be manipulated. If you cannot deconstruct a broker's "income" line into these components, you are taking their word for it — and that is the fastest way to inherit someone else's bad math.

GPR – Gross Potential Rent

Definition

Gross Potential Rent represents the *maximum* rental income a property could generate if every unit was leased at current market rates with no concessions, no vacancy, and perfect collection. It is a "perfect world" number — the theoretical ceiling.

On a **T-12 (Trailing 12-month) income statement**, you might see it labeled as **Market Rent** or **Gross Potential Rent**. On a **rent roll**, it often reflects the "market" rate for each unit type.

Why It Matters

- **Benchmarking**: GPR provides a baseline to measure performance.

- **Market Positioning**: Comparing GPR to actual collections reveals how far below market the property is operating.

- **Value-Add Potential**: A large gap between GPR and current rents can signal an opportunity — but also a risk if the gap exists for good reason (weak demand, over-supply, poor property condition).

Example

Imagine a 100-unit property where market rents are $1,500/month for each unit:

- GPR = 100 × $1,500 × 12 = **$1,800,000/year**.

If you see this on a broker's pro forma, you need to ask: *Is this based on in-place leases or on "aspirational" market comps? (More on comps, a very important topic, later).*

Loss to Lease (LTL)

Definition

Loss to Lease measures the gap between the market rent and the actual rent being collected under signed leases.

Formula:

Loss to Lease = Market Rent – Contract Rent

If the market rent is higher than the rent in existing leases, the result is a **loss to lease** (negative impact on income). If contract rents exceed current market rents, the result is a **gain to lease** (positive impact).

Why It Exists

- **Lease Lag**: In multifamily, most tenants sign 12-month leases. In a rising market, older leases often lag behind current rates.

- **Concessions**: Temporary discounts or incentives lower effective rent even when market rent is higher.

- **Operational Strategy**: An owner may deliberately keep rents slightly below market to maintain high occupancy.

Red Flags

- **Chronic Loss to Lease**: Could indicate a property has trouble moving tenants to market rent.

- **Aggressive Gain to Lease**: If contract rents are significantly above market, tenant retention risk rises — renewals may drop when tenants realize they can rent elsewhere for less.

Example

Market Rent: $1,500/month.
Contract Rent: $1,400/month.
Loss to Lease = $1,500 – $1,400 = $100/month per unit.
For 100 units: $100 × 100 × 12 = **$120,000/year** in lost potential income.

Effective Rent

Definition

Effective Rent is the actual rent collected after accounting for concessions and discounts. It is the truest reflection of what tenants are paying.

Formula:

Effective Rent = Contract Rent – Concessions

This figure is crucial for cash flow projections because it shows what is *really* hitting the bank account.

Why It Matters

- **Cash Flow Reality Check**: GPR may look impressive, but Effective Rent drives the actual dollars you can use to pay expenses and debt.

- **Marketing vs. Operations**: Some operators offer high concessions to attract tenants, inflating occupancy rates but weakening real income.

- **Portfolio Comparison**: Effective Rent is the apples-to-apples figure for comparing properties in different markets.

Example

Contract Rent: $1,400/month.
Concessions: $50/month.
Effective Rent = $1,350/month.
Across 100 units: $1,350 × 100 × 12 = **$1,620,000/year** — a meaningful drop from the $1,800,000/year GPR.

From Theory to Practice – Walking the Numbers

Let's revisit Jane's sample deal property.

Step 1: Start with GPR

Market rent across the property's mix of units: **$2,050,000/ year**.

Step 2: Subtract Loss to Lease

Difference between market rent and in-place leases: **–$180,000/year**.

Step 3: Account for Concessions

Move-in specials and discounts: **–$45,000/year**.

Result – Effective Rent

$2,050,000 – $180,000 – $45,000 = **$1,825,000/year**.

"See that?" Rossi said, circling the bottom line. "If you had underwritten this deal off GPR alone, you'd be overstating income by $225,000. That's not a rounding error — that's the difference between a deal that works and one that bleeds."

Quick Self-Test

- A property has GPR of $1,500,000, Loss to Lease of $75,000, and concessions of $25,000.
  - What is the Effective Rent?
    (Answer: $1,500,000 – $75,000 – $25,000 = $1,400,000)

- Why might a high Gain to Lease be a potential warning sign? *(Answer: It can signal unsustainable rents that risk higher turnover.)*

Best Practices for Evaluating Income Metrics

1. Always Rebuild GPR Yourself

- Use the rent roll and actual unit mix along with rent comps, not broker assumptions.

2. Scrutinize Loss to Lease Trends

- Is it seasonal? Related to lease expirations? Tied to specific floor plans?

3. Quantify Concessions in Dollars and %

- Even small per-unit discounts add up fast.

4. Tie to Market Reality

- Compare to competitive properties in the submarket.

5. Run Sensitivity Scenarios

- Test what happens if LTL narrows more slowly than planned, or if Effective Rent dips due to heavier concessions.

Numbers are not just math — they are the story of a property's performance, past and future. If you can read that story at the top of the income statement, you are already ahead of most investors who skip straight to the "pro forma" returns.

Jane leaned back, a slow grin spreading across her face. "So the next time I see GPR in big bold type, I'm going to dig until I find the real number."

"That," Rossi said, "is the moment you stop buying the dust jacket and start reading the book."

Vacancy, Occupancy, and Other Income Streams

The Illusion of "95% Full"

Jane glanced at the brochure for a 150-unit property. The occupancy rate was splashed across the page in bold blue letters: **95%**.

"That's solid, right?" she asked.

Rossi raised an eyebrow. "Only if those tenants are paying rent. Occupancy is one of the most abused stats in real estate marketing. And it is one of the easiest to misunderstand if you do not know the difference between *physical* and *economic* occupancy."

Why Vacancy Metrics Matter

After income metrics like GPR, Loss to Lease, and Effective Rent, the next critical layer in underwriting is understanding vacancy and occupancy. These numbers determine how much of your "potential" income actually materializes.

The danger? Investors often look only at physical occupancy — the percentage of units filled — without realizing that this number tells you nothing about whether the rent is being collected, or at what level.

Physical Occupancy

Definition

Physical Occupancy = The number of occupied units ÷ Total units.

If a property has 150 units and 142 are leased, the physical occupancy rate is 94.6%.

Why It Matters

Physical occupancy tells you how full the property is — a key indicator for demand and leasing activity.

Its Limitations

- **No payment guarantee**: Tenants might be in units but not paying rent.

- **Can be artificially inflated**: Offering excessive concessions to fill units quickly boosts physical occupancy but can hurt income.

Economic Occupancy

Definition

Economic Occupancy = (Actual Rent Collected ÷ GPR) × 100.

This metric reflects the percentage of *potential* rent that is actually being collected.

Why It Matters

Economic occupancy factors in:

- Concessions

- Bad debt (unpaid rent)

- Non-revenue units (staff apartments, model units)

- Loss to Lease

- Turnover downtime

It is the truer measure of a property's income health.

Example – The Occupancy Trap

With Rossi's help, Jane peeled the onion a layer deeper for the property that reported 95% physical occupancy, only to find out that 10% of those "occupied" units were not paying rent.

Once concessions, staff units, and bad debt were included, **economic occupancy dropped to around 85%.**

That is a massive difference in cash flow — and in the property's ability to cover expenses and debt.

Often the occupancy of a property may be expressed via an opposite term — Vacancy.

Vacancy is the inverse of Occupancy (= 100% -Occupancy %).

Vacancy Types to Watch

1. **Physical Vacancy** – Empty units, whether marketable or under renovation.

2. **Economic Vacancy** – Loss of income from bad debt, concessions, or rent-free units.

3. **Lease-Up Vacancy** – Temporary during initial lease-up of a new or renovated property.

4. **Turnover Vacancy** – Short-term between move-outs and new move-ins.

Vacancy Allowance in Underwriting

When underwriting, you typically apply a vacancy allowance to reflect market norms and lender requirements.

- Agency lenders often assume **5% vacancy** for stabilized properties, even if current vacancy is lower.

- In soft or declining markets, using 8–10% (or higher) is more realistic.

- Heavy value-add properties may require 15%+ during renovations.

- Always check against the long-term occupancy (or vacancy) for the specific market.

Other Income Streams

In addition to rent, multifamily properties generate revenue from ancillary sources. These can make a meaningful difference in NOI if they are recurring, defensible, and in line with market norms.

Common examples:

- Pet fees (monthly and one-time)

- Parking fees (reserved or covered parking)
- Laundry facilities
- Valet trash service
- Utility reimbursements (RUBS)
- Application and late fees
- Storage rentals

Best Practices for Analyzing Other Income

1. Verify Sustainability

- Are fees recurring and market-supported, or one-time and unsustainable?

2. Benchmark Against Competitors

- If a property charges $50/month for parking but no other property in the area does, assume pushback.

3. Check Lease Language

- Are fees properly documented in leases? If not, they may be difficult to enforce.

4. Avoid Double Counting

- Make sure ancillary fees are not already baked into rent projections.

Effective Gross Income (EGI)

To bring this all together, EGI represents Gross Potential Rent - Loss To Lease - Physical Vacancy - Economic Vacancy

+ Other Income. In a typical business, EGI would be the equivalent of net revenue.

Mini Exercise

A property has:

- GPR = $2,000,000.
- Physical occupancy = 95%.
- Bad debt = $60,000.
- Concessions = $20,000.

Question:

What is the economic occupancy?

Solution:

Actual Rent Collected = $2,000,000 – ($100,000 physical vacancy + $60,000 bad debt + $20,000 concessions) = $1,820,000.

Economic Occupancy = $1,820,000 ÷ $2,000,000 = **91%**.

Occupancy is like a fruit basket — it may look abundant, but you need to check if the fruit is fresh or already starting to spoil.

Physical occupancy fills a building.

Economic occupancy fills your bank account.

When you know the difference — and track other income streams honestly — you turn marketing gloss into financial reality.

Operating Expenses and Net Operating Income (NOI)

The Numbers That Sneak Up on You

Jane tapped her pen against the underwriting template. "The rent side makes sense now," she said. "But my NOI is way lower than I expected."

"That," Rossi said, "is because expenses are where bad underwriting hides. Get them wrong, and your NOI will be fiction."

Context – Why Expenses and NOI Are Joined at the Hip

Operating expenses and NOI are not just bookkeeping entries. They are the control levers for a property's profitability, its valuation, and its financing terms.

If GPR, Loss to Lease, and Effective Rent form the *top line* of your income statement, then operating expenses carve their way down to the *bottom line before debt* — Net Operating Income.

Operating Expenses – Definition and Scope

Definition

All costs associated with running and maintaining the property, excluding capital expenditures, debt service, and owner distributions.

Common expense categories:

- **Property Taxes** – Often the single largest expense.

- **Insurance** – Hazard, liability, and sometimes flood or earthquake.

- **Utilities** – Landlord-paid water, gas, electric, trash, internet (if included).

- **Repairs and Maintenance (R&M) and Unit Turns** – Ongoing upkeep and unit turns in between tenants, respectively.

- **Contract Services** – Landscaping, pest control, security, cleaning.

- **Property Management Fees** – Usually a % of effective gross income.

- **Administrative and Marketing Costs** – Office supplies, software, marketing.

- **Replacement Reserves** – Funds set aside for major replacements (roofs, HVAC, etc.), often required by the lender.

Expense Ratios – A Quick Gut Check

Operating expense ratio (OER) = Operating Expenses ÷ Effective Gross Income (EGI).

Typical Ranges for Multifamily:

- 40–45% for large, newer properties.

- 50% or higher for older properties or those in higher-tax/utility markets.

- Outliers below 35% often indicate underreporting or unsustainable cuts. HOWEVER, that depends on the property vintage (age) and market. A brand-new property located in a low property and low insurance state, may be able to operate at 30-40% expense ratio.

Pro Tip: Use expense floors (per unit) in your underwriting too (not only expense ratios). It would be virtually impossible to operate a property at less than $6,000/unit/year. A few common expense ranges include but are not limited to:

- R&M: $500/door/year

- Turns: $300/door/year

- Admin: $300-400/door/year

- Contract services: $300-500/door/year

- Marketing: $50-150/door/year

When adding taxes, insurance, utilities, and property management/payroll, the expenses can quickly add up to $6,000 or above.

The NOI Equation

Formula:

NOI = Effective Gross Income – Operating Expenses

NOI represents the property's operating profit *before* financing and taxes. It is the key driver for:

- **Valuation** (Value = NOI ÷ Cap Rate).

- **Debt Sizing** (Lenders use NOI to calculate Debt Service Coverage and Debt Yield).

- **Return Metrics** (Cash-on-Cash, IRR, Equity Multiple).

Example – From Rent Roll to NOI

Effective Gross Income: $1,820,000.

Operating Expenses: $900,000.

NOI = $1,820,000 – $900,000 = **$920,000.**

At a 6% cap rate:

Value ≈ $920,000 ÷ 0.06 = **$15.33MM.**

If expenses were understated by just $50,000, NOI would drop to $870,000, reducing value by more than **$830,000** at the same cap rate.

Expense Red Flags in Underwriting

1. **Omitted Line Items** – No reserve for replacements or unrealistically low R&M.

2. **Tax Assumptions** – Not adjusting for post-sale reassessment (common in high-tax states, more on that in Chapter 6).

3. **Management Fees** – Using below-market % to pad NOI.

4. **Utility Reimbursements** – Assuming 100% recovery without lease or market proof.

5. **One-Time Discounts** – Lower insurance premiums in Year 1 that will normalize upward.

The Analysis Drill

Jane stared at the offering memorandum. "The expense ratio is 35%. That's great, right?"

Rossi chuckled. "Not unless this property is magic. They are missing reserves, admin costs, and they have taxes locked at the seller's rate. After reassessment, expenses will jump — and NOI will drop. You do not want to find that out after closing."

Best Practices for Expense Underwriting

- **Use Historical + Market Data** – Blend T-12 with realistic pro forma adjustments.

- **Apply Per-Door Minimums** – Prevents overly optimistic estimates.

- **Adjust for Property Age/Condition** – Older assets cost more to maintain.

- **Stress Test Taxes and Insurance** – Especially in volatile markets.

- **Confirm Service Contracts** – Actual terms, not just budget placeholders.

Exercise:

A property's Effective Gross Income is $2,400,000.Operating Expenses are 48% of EGI.

- What is the NOI? *(Answer: $2,400,000 × (100%-48%) = $1,248,000)*.

- At a 6.25% cap rate, what is the implied value? *(Answer: $1,248,000 ÷ 0.0625 = $19,968,000)*.

NOI is more than a number — it is the heartbeat of your investment. Every dollar of expenses you miss in underwriting is a dollar less in NOI, a multiplied loss in valuation, and a potential deal-breaker.Learn to see expenses not as a chore to estimate, but as the key to uncovering the property's *true* worth.

Jane closed her laptop. "I get it now. The math is simple, but the discipline is in the assumptions."

"Exactly," Rossi said. "That discipline is what separates speculators from investors."

Cap Rate — One of The Most Controversial Metrics

One Metric, a Thousand Opinions

"Cap rate," Jane said slowly, "is just NOI divided by purchase price, right?"

Rossi grinned. "Yes. And no. That's the formula, but cap rates are also the most argued-over number in commercial real estate. Get it wrong, and your valuation — and your entire deal — can fall apart."

Context – Why Cap Rates Matter

Cap rates, or capitalization rates, are the most common shorthand for valuing income-producing property. They connect the property's income (NOI) to its market value and give investors, appraisers, and lenders a way to compare opportunities across markets and asset classes. You can think of it as an inverse multiplier used to value the property.

Formula:

Cap Rate = NOI ÷ Purchase Price

Rearranged for valuation:

Value = NOI ÷ Cap Rate

What Cap Rates Really Represent

- **Unlevered Return**: The rate of return if you bought the property with all cash. It is a universal metric used to compare across properties, as not all properties have the same debt structure and not all may be leveraged.

- **Risk Premium**: The extra return you demand above a "risk-free" investment like the 10-year Treasury.

- **Market Sentiment Gauge**: Lower cap rates indicate stronger demand and higher prices; higher cap rates suggest weaker demand or perceived risk.

What Drives Cap Rates

Cap rates are influenced by:

- **Macroeconomics** – Interest rates, inflation expectations, capital flows.

- **Local Market Conditions** – Job growth, population trends, supply/demand for housing.

- **Asset-Specific Factors** – Class (A/B/C), age, condition, tenant base, amenities.

- **Investor Competition** – More buyers chasing fewer assets drives cap rates down (prices up).

Example:

- A Class A property in Dallas may trade at a 4.75% cap.

- A Class C property in a tertiary market may trade at an 8% cap.

This does not mean that the Class C property is necessarily better, just because it has a higher cap rate (or higher unlevered return). If anything, it carries more risk due to the property class and market location.

Cap Rate Compression and Expansion

- **Compression**: Cap rates fall as prices rise faster than income — often in hot markets or when debt is cheap.

- **Expansion (aka reversion)**: Cap rates rise when perceived risk increases, income growth slows, or borrowing costs climb.

Even small changes have big impacts. A 50-basis-point change in cap rate can move valuation by hundreds of thousands — or millions — of dollars.

Example:

A property generating $100,000 NOI at a 5% cap rate, would be valued at $2,000,000.

That same property generating $100,000 NOI at a 6% cap rate, would be valued at $1,666,667 (a 17% decrease in value).

That same property generating $100,000 NOI at a 4% cap rate, would be valued at $2,500,00 (a 25% increase in value).

Why Conservative Assumptions Matter

In pro forma underwriting, cap rates are often assumed to be stable or even lower at exit. **That is dangerous.**

- **Reality Check**: If you buy at a 5.25% cap, model at least 10 bps per year higher at the time of exit. For example, if you hold that same property for 5 years, the exit cap rate at sale would be 5.75% (model a higher increase than 10 bps per year in a rising interest rate environment).

- **Market Cycles**: Rising interest rates, recession fears, or oversupply can quickly push cap rates upward.

- **Downside Protection**: Conservative cap rate growth assumptions protect your IRR if market sentiment shifts.

Example – The 50-Bps Surprise

Jane's model assumed a 5% exit cap on a $1,000,000 NOI, valuing the sale at $20MM.

If the exit cap rises to 5.5%, that same NOI yields a value of $18.18MM — nearly $2MM less.

"That's why," Rossi said, "we never count on cap rate compression. If the deal only works with a lower cap rate in the future, it's not a deal — it's a bet."

Cap Rate vs. Interest Rate – The Leverage Signal

If the cap rate is lower than your loan interest rate, you have **negative leverage** — the cost of capital (debt) exceeds the unlevered rate of return. This is a strong indicator that the property might not cash flow. It also suggests that from an investor's perspective, it is best if it is bought all cash.

If the cap rate is higher than your interest rate, you have **positive leverage** — debt boosts returns.

This interplay ties directly into Yield on Cost and Debt Service Coverage, which we cover shortly.

Market Spread Perspective

Historically, apartment cap rates have averaged about 200 basis points above the 10-year Treasury (the spread fluctuates during periods of expansion or contraction).

- Narrow spreads = more aggressive pricing and thinner margins.

- Wide spreads = potentially better buying opportunities.

But spreads are not perfectly correlated — cap rates can stay low even when rates rise if investors still see multifamily as a safe haven.

Best Practices for Cap Rate Underwriting

1. **Use Market-Specific Data** – Pull actual comps from recent sales, not national averages (appraisals, the CoStar underwriting report, and brokers are great sources for this type of data).

2. **Segment by Asset Class** – A Class C in a workforce housing submarket will not trade at the same cap as a luxury midrise.

3. **Apply Exit Cap Rate Expansion from Current Market Cap Rate Levels** – Model 10 bps per year higher for each year the property is held for risk cushion (or higher in a rising interest rate environment).

4. **Stress Test** – Run scenarios with higher cap rates and see if returns still meet your targets.

5. **Align with Debt Terms** – Check if your cap rate supports positive leverage.

Exercise

You buy a property with NOI of $750,000 at a 6% cap.

1. What is the purchase price? *(Answer: $750,000 ÷ 0.06 = $12.5MM)*.

2. If the exit cap is 6.5% with the same NOI, what is the sale price? *(Answer: $750,000 ÷ 0.065 = $11.54MM)*.

3. How much value is lost? *(Answer: $960,000)*.

Debrief

Jane leaned back. "So, the cap rate is more than just a math formula. It's a market mood ring."

"Exactly," Rossi said. "And moods change. Conservative assumptions keep you from overpaying when the music stops."

Cap rates are not crystal balls, but they are compasses. They tell you where the market is pointing today — and hint at where risk may lie tomorrow.

Underwrite them with caution, question every assumption, and never forget: in multifamily investing, the price you pay is the foundation for every return you hope to earn.

Yield On Cost (YOC) – Cap Rate's Cousin

What It Is and Why It Matters

The unlevered rate of return on an asset based on the *all-in cost* to acquire the asset.

Calculated as Stabilized NOI divided by the All-In Cost of a Property (All-In Cost of a Property = Purchase Price + Capex + Closing Costs).

Applicable to value-add projects (and new development deals) and often preferred over cap rate, as it captures the full cost involved with repositioning the asset.

Exercise

You buy a property with stabilized NOI of $750,000, closing costs of $300,000, capex of $500,000, and purchase price of $10,000,000.

1. What is the yield on cost? *(Answer: $750,000 ÷ ($10,000,000+$500,000+$300,000) = 6.9%.*

2. If the loan all-in interest rate is 6.0%, is leverage positive or negative? *(Answer: Positive as 6.9% YOC > 6.0% all-in rate on the loan).*

Debt Metrics: Debt Service Coverage, Debt Yield, and Leverage

When the Bank Says "No"

Jane frowned at the lender's term sheet. "But our loan request was at 75% LTV (Loan to Value). That's fine, right?"

Rossi shook her head. "Not if the cash flow cannot support it. Lenders are not just looking at how much you borrow (LTV) — they are looking at how safely you can pay it back. That's where debt metrics come in."

Why Debt Metrics Matter

Debt metrics are the bridge between a property's performance and the financing you can secure. They dictate:

- Whether you get the loan.

- How much you can borrow.

- What covenants you will live with during the loan term.

The two primary cash flow metrics lenders use — and that sophisticated investors track — are **Debt Service Coverage (DSC)** and **Debt Yield (DY)**. Each measures risk from a slightly different angle.

Debt Service Coverage (DSC)

Definition

Debt Service Coverage Ratio =
NOI ÷ Annual Debt Service (Principal + Interest)

It measures how many times the property's net operating income can cover the annual loan payments.

Why It Matters

- **Lender Risk Gauge**: Low DSC means less cushion — if income drops, payments may not be met.

- **Loan Sizing Tool**: Lenders size the loan to meet their minimum DSC requirement.

- **Investor Risk Signal**: DSC under 1.0 means the property cannot fully pay its debt service with cash flow from operations.

Typical Standards

- Lenders: 1.25x minimum for stabilized multifamily (this number varies based on the lender and the operator/property/deal/market risk profile).

- Conservative operators target 1.50–1.60x to allow for some cushion and reduce the risk of covenant default.

- Watch out if DSC < 1.0 — it means negative cash flow after debt service.

Example

NOI = $900,000.

Debt Service = $600,000.

DSC = 900,000 ÷ 600,000 = **1.50x.**

This means NOI covers debt service 1.5 times, leaving a 50% cushion.

Debt Yield (DY)

Definition

Debt Yield = NOI ÷ Loan Amount

Expressed as a percentage, it represents how quickly the loan principal would be paid by current NOI, all else equal, and if the lender owned the property outright. You can think of it as an inverse cash flow leverage metric.

Why It Matters

- **Pure Risk Measure**: Independent of interest rate or amortization schedule.

- **Downside Protection**: Shows how quickly the loan could be repaid if the lender took over, all else equal.

- **Loan Limit Tool**: Some lenders cap loan size based on minimum DY.

Typical Standards

- Many lenders target ≥10% DY for multifamily.

- Lower DY = higher leverage and higher risk.

Example

NOI = $900,000.
Loan Amount = $9,000,000.
Debt Yield = 900,000 ÷ 9,000,000 = **10%.**

If DY drops below the lender's threshold and depending on how the loan is structured, they may require a loan pay down (especially if DSC is rocky too).

DSC vs. Debt Yield – The Key Difference

- DSC looks at *income vs. debt payments.*

- Debt Yield looks at *income vs. loan size.*

A property could meet DSC requirements because of low interest rates but still fail DY, if the leverage is too high.

Real-World Case – The DY Curveball

From Rossi's own lender experience:

An investor expected a $12MM loan at 75% LTV.

- NOI: $1,200,000.

- At 4.5% interest, DSC = 1.35x (acceptable).

- But Debt Yield = 1,200,000 ÷ 12,000,000 = 10%.

The lender's policy minimum was 10.5% — so they reduced the loan amount to $11.43MM, surprising the investor.

"That's why," Rossi told Jane, "We review both DSC and DY before even calling the bank."

Best Practices for Investors

1. **Run Both Metrics Early** – Avoid surprises late in the financing process.

2. **Know Lender Thresholds** – Agency, bridge, and bank lenders have different minimums.

3. **Model Interest Rate Stress** – A 1–2% rate hike can crush DSC.

4. **Track DY Post-Close** – Falling NOI or increased leverage (refi, supplemental loan) can trigger covenant issues.

5. **Use DY as a Sanity Check** – Even without lender input, it helps you avoid over-leveraging.

Exercise

A property's NOI is $1,000,000.

- Annual debt service = $700,000.

- Loan amount = $10,500,000.

1. What is DSC? *(Answer: 1,000,000 ÷ 700,000 = 1.43x).*

2. What is Debt Yield? *(Answer: 1,000,000 ÷ 10,500,000 ≈ 9.52%).*

3. Would a lender with a 10% DY minimum approve full funding? *(Answer: No — loan size would need to be reduced by $500,000).*

The Conversation Continued

Jane said, "I used to think LTV was the only thing that mattered."

"That's what most new investors think," Rossi replied. "But lenders want to know two things: how much income covers the debt (DSC), and how much income covers the loan size (DY). Both protect them — and both should protect you."

Lenders are not the enemy — they are your first line of due diligence (and your largest capital partner). When you speak their language and run their metrics before they do, you gain leverage in negotiations and clarity in your investment decisions.

Strong DSC and DY do not just get you the loan. They help ensure the loan is one you will still be glad you have when the market changes.

Break-Even Occupancy and Stress Testing

How Low Can You Go?

Jane scrolled through the underwriting model. "So, if occupancy drops, when do we start losing money?"

"That," Rossi said, "is exactly what break-even occupancy tells you. It's the 'how far can we fall before we're underwater' number. And every serious investor should know it before making an offer."

Context – The Cushion Between Profit and Loss

Break-even occupancy answers one of the most critical risk questions in multifamily investing:

- At what occupancy level do revenues just cover operating expenses and debt service — with nothing left over?

Knowing this number is not just for lenders. It is a tool for gauging how resilient your investment will be in downturns, lease-up periods, or unexpected events.

Break-Even Occupancy – The Basics

Formula (Traditional):

Break-Even Occupancy (%) = (Operating Expenses + Debt Service) ÷ Gross Potential Rent

This measures the percentage of *gross potential* rent you need to cover all costs.

Modified Break-Even (preferred calculation method):

Break-Even Ratio (%) = (Operating Expenses + Debt Service) ÷ Effective Gross Income

This version includes the impact of economic vacancy and other income streams, and is often preferred by lenders.

Why It Matters

- **Risk Cushion**: A lower break-even occupancy means more buffer before losses.

- **Market Resilience**: In a downturn, properties with high break-even requirements are more vulnerable.

Example – Interpreting the Number

A 100-unit property has:

- Effective Gross Income: $1,800,000/year.

- Operating Expenses: $720,000/year.

- Debt Service: $600,000/year.

Break-Even Occupancy =

= ($720,000 + $600,000) ÷ $1,800,000
= $1,320,000 ÷ $1,800,000 = **73.3%.**

This means occupancy could drop to roughly 73% or EGI can drop by 27% before the property stops covering costs.

Typical Ranges

- **Strong**: ≤ 70%
- **Watchlist**: 70-80%
- **Risky**: ≥ 80% (very little cushion)

Investors should aim for no more than break-even of 80% (preferably less than that) for safety.

Stress Testing – Your Investment Safety Net

Break-even is only the starting point. Stress testing pushes your underwriting model through "what if" scenarios:

1. **Occupancy Drops** – Model 5–10% lower occupancy than pro forma.

2. **Rent Softens** – Reduce market rent by $50–100/unit.

3. **Expenses Spike** – Increase taxes, insurance, or utilities by 10–20%.

4. **Debt Costs Rise** – Add 100–200 basis points to your interest rate (if floating).

Goal: The deal still meets minimum DSC, debt yield, beak even-occupancy, and cash flow requirements under stress conditions.

The Walkthrough

Jane ran the numbers on a promising deal. Break-even came out at 88%.

"That's not terrible," she said.

Rossi shook her head. "That means if you lose just 12% of paying tenants — which can happen in a soft market — you're at zero cash flow. One big insurance hike or tax reassessment, and you're negative."

Jane adjusted the model. At 80% break-even, the property felt far more defensible.

Best Practices for Break-Even & Stress Testing

- **Run Both Versions**: Traditional (GPR-based) and modified (EGI-based).

- **Match to Market Volatility**: In cyclical markets, demand a bigger cushion.

- **Make It Routine**: Stress test every deal before LOI — not after due diligence.

- **Layer the Tests**: Combine multiple stress factors for worst-case modeling.

Exercise

You have:

- EGI: $2,000,000.

- Operating Expenses: $900,000.

- Debt Service: $700,000.

Question 1: What is break-even occupancy?
(Answer: ($900,000 + $700,000) ÷ $2,000,000 = 80%).

Question 2: If rents drop by 5%, what happens to break-even?
(Answer: EGI falls to $1,900,000, making break-even ≈ 84.2% — less cushion).

Break-even occupancy is your early warning system. It tells you how far the property can bend before it breaks.

When paired with stress testing, it transforms your underwriting from a single optimistic forecast into a range of possible futures — some comfortable, some uncomfortable.

And in those uncomfortable futures, you will already know the plan.

Rossi leaned back. "Deals don't fail because nothing goes wrong. They fail because no one planned for when things did. Break-even and stress tests are how you plan for *when*, not *if*."

Key Return Metrics: Cash-on-Cash, IRR, and Equity Multiple

The "Investor's Scoreboard"

Jane slid her underwriting model across the table. "So… this is where I figure out if the deal is worth it?"

Rossi nodded. "Exactly. These are the investor's scorecards — the metrics that tell you if the property will deliver the returns you want, in the time frame you want, with the risk you can live with."

Why Return Metrics Matter

While NOI, cap rate, and debt metrics reveal a property's operational and financing health, return metrics translate those numbers into investor outcomes. They answer three big questions:

1. How much cash will I receive relative to what I invest?

2. How quickly will I get my money back?

3. How much will I have at the end compared to what I started with?

The "big three" most investors focus on are **Cash-on-Cash Return (CoC)**, **Internal Rate of Return (IRR)**, and **Equity Multiple (EM)**.

Cash-on-Cash Return (CoC)

Definition

Cash-on-Cash Return measures the annual pre-tax cash flow as a percentage of the total cash invested. It shows the income yield relative to your out-of-pocket equity.

Formula:

CoC = Annual Pre-Tax Cash Flow ÷ Total Equity Invested

Why It Matters

- Immediate yield — tells you what your money is earning *this year.*

- Helps compare real estate to other income-focused investments (on a pre-tax basis).

- Sensitive to financing structure, operating efficiency, and reserve policies.

Example

If you invest $500,000 and the property distributes $40,000 in year one:

CoC = $40,000 ÷ $500,000 = **8%.**

Rossi's note to Jane: "Strong CoC is nice, but make sure it's sustainable — not boosted by inflated rents or unrealistic expense assumptions."

Internal Rate of Return (IRR)

Definition

IRR is the discount rate at which the present value of future cash flows (including sale proceeds) equals the original investment. In simpler terms, it is the annualized rate of return factoring in both timing and amount of cash flows and the time value of money.

Why It Matters

- Accounts for the *time value of money.*
- More comprehensive than CoC — includes both operating income and capital events (refinance, sale).
- Useful for comparing deals of different durations.

Limitations

- Can be manipulated by front-loading returns or using aggressive exit assumptions.
- Assumes reinvestment of interim cash flows at the IRR rate — often unrealistic.

Example

If $500,000 grows to $800,000 over 5 years with varying annual cash flows, the IRR is about ~9.5%.

Jane learned that a slightly longer hold or slower exit could drag IRR down — even if total profit stayed the same.

Equity Multiple (EM)

Definition

Equity Multiple = Total Cash Received ÷ Total Cash Invested.

It measures how many times over you've multiplied your original equity by the end of the investment.

Why It Matters

- Simple "total return" measure — no time value assumption.

- Great for understanding scale of profit in long-term deals.

- Useful when combined with IRR to assess *magnitude vs. speed*.

Example

If you invest $500,000 and over 5 years receive $900,000 in distributions and gain on sale proceeds:

EM = $900,000 ÷ $500,000 = **1.8x.**

How These Metrics Work Together

Scenario A:

- CoC: 9%
- IRR: 15%
- EM: 1.9x
- Break-Even: 85%

High income, strong total return — but higher vulnerability if occupancy dips.

Scenario B:

- CoC: 7%
- IRR: 14%
- EM: 1.8x
- Break-Even: 78%

Slightly lower income and total return — but greater resilience in downturns.

Lesson: Strong underwriting balances return metrics with risk tolerance.

Exercise

You invest $250,000 in a deal that returns:

- Year 1–4: $20,000/year in distributions.
- Year 5: $20,000 distributions + $300,000 sale proceeds.

1. What is the total EM?
   (Answer: 4 x $20,000 + $20,000 + $300,000 = $400,000 total cash received; $400,000÷ $250,000 = 1.60x EM).

2. If the hold is shortened to 4 years with the same total return, what happens to IRR?
   (Answer: IRR rises because capital is returned faster).

Debrief

Jane leaned over her spreadsheet. "So CoC tells me my yearly paycheck, IRR tells me my annualized return including the sale, EM tells me my total profit, and break-even tells me how much trouble I can survive."

Rossi smiled. "Exactly. And the best investors never look at just one of them — they read all four together."

Mastering these return metrics equips you to speak the language of both operators and investors, compare deals intelligently, and spot when numbers are being spun to look better than they are.

Equipped with a firm understanding of the key terminology and concepts, Jane is now ready to dive into the full financial analysis of the property — where these metrics come alive in real-world underwriting.

CHAPTER 6

THE FIVE-STEP UNDERWRITING FRAMEWORK (INCLUDING FULL FINANCIAL ANALYSIS)

Step 1: Income Analysis and Rent Comps

The Most Dangerous Number in Multifamily Underwriting

One of the two most dangerous numbers to get wrong in a multifamily deal is not the purchase price (though getting that right and not overpaying is important, and we'll cover how to minimize the risk of overpaying as we move through this chapter…in fact this first step we are about to discuss is key).

It is getting the rents wrong.

Why? Because rent assumptions sit at the very top of the pro forma. Overestimate them and you are building your entire deal on a foundation that is already cracking. Every single income-driven metric – Net Operating Income, debt coverage, value, projected returns – will be inflated. In addition, as you start forecasting from the base rent, the number compounds over time, which can amplify the issue if not done right from the start.

A deal that looks flawless on paper can quickly crumble within twelve months because the actual market rents come in $75 lower than projected. On a 200-unit property, that is $180,000 a year in lost revenue – enough to wipe out a material amount of the cash flow and trigger investor anxiety.

That is why Step 1 in the five-step underwriting blueprint starts here: validating the income, and specifically, testing the rent assumptions against reality.

Why Rent Comps Matter More Than You Think

Back when Rossi Monroe first sat down with Jane to review her first full multifamily deal, she did not start with cap rates, financing structures, or the return profile. She started with one deceptively simple question:

"How do you know those rents are accurate?"

Jane hesitated. The sponsor's deck had a neat table with "market rent comps" – all higher than the property's current rates. The broker had even added glossy photos of nearby apartments to prove it.

Rossi smiled. "That is not enough. You cannot take someone else's homework and assume they got the answer right. You have to check the work."

That is the essence of income analysis – removing the optimism, the marketing gloss, and the wishful thinking, and grounding your pro forma in data that stands up to scrutiny.

The Four-Part Rent Comp Framework

Accurate rent analysis is part art, part science. The science comes from data – comparable properties, current asking rents, actual signed leases. The art comes from context – knowing which comps are truly comparable and how concessions, amenities, and property condition affect pricing power.

Here is the framework Rossi walked Jane through:

1. Identify True Comparable Properties

Your goal is not just to find "apartments in the same city." It is to find properties that a tenant would reasonably consider as an alternative to your subject property.

Key filters:

- **Location proximity** – Ideally within one mile in urban areas; expand to 3–5 miles in suburban areas (or more in rural or less densely populated areas).

- **Property age and construction type** – A 1980s Class C property is not competing directly with a 2020 luxury high-rise Class A property.

- **Unit mix and size** – A 750 sq. ft. one-bedroom is not equivalent to a 550 sq. ft. studio.

- **Condition and finish level** – Classic interiors, partial renovations, or full upgrades will all rent at different levels.

- **Amenities** – Pools, gyms, in-unit laundry, parking – each can justify a price difference.

A frequent rookie mistake is to accept broker-provided comps without testing these filters. If the "market rent" they cite is based on properties that are newer, better located, or more upgraded, you are overestimating your achievable rent from day one.

2. Verify Rents Using Multiple Sources

Do not rely on a single data point – especially not just the offering memorandum. Cross-check with:

- **Third-party listing sites** – Apartments.com, Apartment List, Rentometer (note: these sites show *asking* rents, not net effective rents).

- **Property management contacts** – They often have live, on-the-ground leasing data.

- **CoStar or Yardi reports** – Subscription-based, but invaluable if you have access.

- **Secret shopping** – Call as a prospective tenant or hire someone local to tour and report back.

- **Public records and loan packages** – Sometimes appraisals or lender reports reveal in-place rents.

Rossi's tip to Jane: "Always confirm with at least two independent sources. If they disagree, dig deeper until you know why."

3. Adjust for Concessions and Net Effective Rent

A unit listed at $1,500 a month with "one month free" is not really a $1,500 unit. That incentive drops the net effective rent to $1,375 over a 12-month lease.

This is where many novice underwriters miss the mark. Listing sites rarely show concessions clearly. You need to ask property managers directly or track specials advertised in leasing offices.

For example, in one Dallas deal, the sponsor projected rent growth based on "market comps" that appeared $100 above current in-place rents. On closer inspection, Rossi found that every single comp was running heavy concessions – equivalent to $80–$90 off monthly. The "rent gap" essentially vanished.

4. Validate Rent Growth Assumptions

Even if your starting rent numbers are accurate, growth assumptions can make or break your model.

In a stable market, conservative growth might be 2–3% annually. In a softening market, zero or even negative growth in Year 1 may be prudent.

Rossi's rule: "Match growth assumptions to market momentum as well as the long run historical average rate for that market (this is exactly why we started with the market first before diving into the numbers), not wishful thinking." If job growth is slow, supply is high, affordability is low, or absorption is weak, you cannot force rent growth without sacrificing occupancy.

Other Income: Often Overlooked, Sometimes Overstated

In addition to base rent, you will see "other income" in most pro formas – pet rent, parking fees, laundry, rubs (utility reimbursements). While these can boost revenue, they need scrutiny too.

Positive contributors (aka accretive other income line items) include pet rent or reserved parking fees. Negative "other income" sources – like late fees or eviction charges – may indicate operational or tenant quality issues (aka dilutive other income line items). A heavy reliance on these is a red flag.

When evaluating other income, it is also important to consider local demand. For example, if all properties allow pets and charge pet rent, it is reasonable to assume that adding that income stream will enhance marketability of the property. Conversely, adding valet trash services in a market where tenants do not want or need such service only makes the proforma look great on paper but result in zero valet trash fees actually generated.

Pulling It Together: Jane's First Income Analysis

In the case study Jane and Rossi worked through, the sponsor projected average rents of $1,450, with "market comps" at $1,525–$1,550.

Jane followed the framework:

- She narrowed the comps from six broker-provided properties to three that matched in age, location, and amenities.

- She secret-shopped all three, discovering that one had a "first month free" promotion and another offered a $500 gift card at move-in.

- After adjusting for concessions, the *true* market average was $1,465 – barely above current in-place rents.

By making this adjustment, Jane's underwriting dropped the projected Year 1 NOI by $35,000 – enough to change the deal from "tight but okay" to "not worth pursuing."

Practical Tips for Your Own Income Analysis

1. Document your sources – Keep screenshots, emails, and notes for every rent comp.

2. Check seasonality – Rents may swing between summer leasing peaks and winter lulls.

3. Avoid over-reliance on new construction comps – They may not be sustainable benchmarks.

4. Talk to multiple property managers – Especially leasing agents, not just executives or business development staff.

5. Update your analysis close to LOI signing – Markets shift fast; a 60-day-old rent survey may already be outdated.

6. Last but not least, ensure that physical and economic occupancy projections align with the market's historical average and account for an adequate stabilization period. For larger properties, e.g., 150+ units, such period could be 2-3 years (depending on the amount of value add planned). For smaller properties, e.g., 20 units, it could be 12 – 18 months.

The Big Takeaway

If you get the income wrong, nothing else you underwrite will be right.

That is why Step 1 is not just about pulling a few numbers. It is about developing the discipline to question every assumption, cross-check every source, and anchor your projections in reality.

Rossi's final words to Jane before they moved on:

> "This step is where you earn your confidence. If your income numbers are bulletproof, the rest of the analysis will stand on solid ground. But if they are shaky, the whole deal will feel shaky – and it should."

Step 2: Expense Validation

When the Bottom Line is Built on Sand

It is easy to get dazzled by the top line of a pro forma. Those rent numbers look solid, the other income streams add a nice boost, and the Net Operating Income (NOI) seems healthy. But there is a danger hiding in plain sight: understated expenses.

A deal can collapse even when rents come in exactly as projected if the operating expenses have been underestimated. The problem is subtle but deadly — every dollar you miss here is a dollar less in NOI, and because NOI drives valuation, a shortfall compounds the damage.

I once reviewed a Class B property in Texas, *Rossi recalled*, that showed an operating expense ratio (OER) of 35% in the broker's marketing package. The market average for similar properties was 45–50%. On paper, the property looked like a high-efficiency gem. In reality, taxes were about to be reassessed, insurance premiums were climbing, and payroll was understated. When we normalized expenses to realistic levels, NOI dropped by 15%, wiping out most of the projected cash flow.

This is why Step 2 in the five-step underwriting blueprint is Expense Validation. You are not just "checking" numbers — you are pressure-testing them until you are confident they can hold up in real-world conditions.

Jane's First Red Flag

When Jane sat down with Rossi Monroe for their underwriting session, she felt confident. Step 1 — Income Analysis — had been grueling but satisfying. She had stripped away inflated rent comps and adjusted for concessions until she knew her top line was rock-solid.

Now Rossi asked her to scroll down the pro forma.

"What's the OER here?" Rossi asked.

"Thirty-eight percent," Jane replied, glancing at the summary.

Rossi raised an eyebrow. "And what is the market average for this property type and market?"

Jane checked her notes. "Around forty-five percent."

"That's a problem," Rossi said. "If expenses are below market norms without a clear operational reason, you need to assume they will revert to reality."

This was Jane's introduction to expense normalization — the art and science of replacing marketing-friendly numbers with defensible, market-based figures.

The Four-Step Expense Validation Process

1. Normalize Operating Expenses

Start with the property's historical financials — ideally a T12 (trailing twelve months).

- Look for volatility – Are certain expenses unusually low in recent months? This might be seasonal or it might be deferral (e.g., skipping maintenance to boost NOI before sale).

- Adjust for new ownership realities – Some owners self-manage, avoid payroll, or defer capital needs. Under new ownership, these savings may disappear. Taxes will get re-assessed. Insurance will likely increase. The new owner may have to spend more on marketing, especially if they plan on raising rents.

- Apply industry benchmarks – Lenders often have minimum expense expectations (e.g., $6,000–$7,000 per unit per year in total operating expenses, excluding taxes, insurance, and reserves) and compare those to market data via appraisals or the CoStar underwriting report.

If actual expenses fall below these benchmarks, adjust them upward unless you have hard evidence the lower costs are sustainable.

2. Validate Major Line Items

Every major category deserves its own check. Here are the ones that most often require adjustment:

Taxes – One of the easiest to understate and one of the most dangerous to ignore. In many states, a property sale triggers a reassessment based on the purchase price.

- Use the county's property appraiser or tax assessor site to find the current assessed value and millage rate.

- Apply the reassessment rate based on the purchase price. In some counties properties are reassessed at 40%. In others — at 80%.

- If unsure or if the information is not available online, call the assessor's office — they can confirm timelines, reassessment %, and reassessment triggers for that specific county.

- Example: In the Texas case study, the sponsor left taxes at the seller's lower assessed value. Once reassessed, the tax bill would have jumped 25%, erasing $50,000 in NOI.

Insurance – Premiums vary by market, property age, and risk profile (flood, wind, fire zones).

- Get a broker's insurance quote early in underwriting — do not rely on the seller's historical rate.

- Compare to recent comps in similar asset types.

- Watch for special coverage needs (e.g., named storm coverage in hurricane-prone markets).

Payroll – Especially in smaller properties, sellers may understate payroll by doing work themselves or underpaying staff.

- Benchmark payroll by unit count and service level (full-time maintenance, leasing staff, etc.). Property managers or Costar would be a good starting point to obtain such benchmarks.

- In many markets, $1,200–$1,800 per unit annually is a starting point.

Repairs & Maintenance (R&M) – The industry floor is often around $500 per unit annually, but older assets may (and likely will) require more.

- Look for sudden drops in R&M before sale — a sign of deferred upkeep.

Turns & Unit Renovations – Turning a unit between tenants costs money. Even light turns average $300–$500 per unit annually.

- Heavy turns or value-add renovations require separate CapEx budgeting, not just operating expense allocation.

Marketing & Advertising – Budget at least $50–$100 per unit annually. If the property shows $0, dig deeper — they may rely on outdated word-of-mouth instead of competitive marketing.

Administrative – Often $300+ per unit annually. This covers office supplies, software, legal, etc.

Contract Services – Landscaping, pest control, security — rarely free. Budget at least $300-500 per unit annually unless proven otherwise.

Utilities – Adjust for seasonal fluctuations and pending rate changes. Confirm whether water/sewer, trash, or other utilities are owner-paid or tenant-reimbursed.

3. Apply Line Item Floors and Ratios

Experienced underwriters (and lenders) use "floors" — minimum per-unit amounts or ratios for each expense category. Your underwriting should too.

For example:

- Operating Expense Ratio (OER) – Minimum 45-50% of EGI in most markets.

- R&M – $500/unit/year minimum.

- Turns – $300/unit/year minimum.

- Marketing – $50–$100/unit/year.

- Admin – $300/unit/year.

- Contract Services – $300/unit/year.

If a pro forma comes in below these, adjust upward unless you have verified, sustainable reasons.

4. Stress-Test for Future Volatility

Even if current expenses are accurate, build in margin for:

- Tax increases – Assume reassessment to purchase price plus modest annual growth consistent with that market.

- Insurance spikes – In some markets, 15–20% annual jumps are not unusual after storms or major claims.

- Utility inflation – Factor in energy price trends and regulatory changes.

Jane's Expense Adjustment in Action

In the Texas deal example, Jane found:

- Taxes understated by $48,000 post-reassessment.

- Insurance likely to rise 12% based on broker quotes.

- Payroll missing a leasing agent's salary.

- R&M well below the $500/unit/year floor.

After normalizing, the OER rose from 38% to 49%. NOI dropped by $90,000 — enough to lower the property value by over $1.5 million at the market cap rate.

Rossi's takeaway for Jane:

> "The seller's job is to make the property look as profitable as possible. Your job is to see through that — and make it realistic. A deal that only works with underwritten expenses is not a deal."

Practical Tips for Expense Validation

1. Use the T12 and T3 together – T12 shows trends; T3 reveals recent shifts (for non-seasonal and non-one-time expenses only).

2. Ask "why" for every variance – If a line item changes significantly year-to-year, get the story.

3. Cross-check with PMs and contractors – They will know realistic costs in your market.

4. Account for property age – Older properties generally have higher R&M and utilities.

5. Budget for compliance – Fire safety, ADA, and local inspection requirements can add hidden costs.

Now that you have a realistic picture of both income and expenses, you can trust your NOI. But even the best projections cannot prevent the unexpected. Roofs leak. Boilers fail. Tenants move out early. That is why Step 3: Reserve Analysis exists — to make sure you have the liquidity to absorb shocks without derailing the deal.

As Rossi told Jane:

"We validate expenses so we know what it costs to run the property. We build reserves so we can survive what we cannot predict."

Step 3: Reserve Analysis

The Silent Protector in Multifamily Underwriting

When deals go wrong, the headlines almost always focus on revenue shortfalls or debt issues. Rarely does the conversation start with reserves — but more often than not, a well-funded reserve account is the difference between riding out a storm and making a desperate capital call.

In my years as both a lender and an investor, *Rossi shared*, I have seen reserves framed as an afterthought. Some sponsors will tell you they keep "a couple of months of expenses" on hand, as though that is a sign of prudence. Others treat reserves as a deal killer because they dilute projected returns. But in reality, reserves are not an optional cushion — they are an operating necessity.

A property is a living, breathing business. Roofs leak, HVAC systems fail in the hottest week of summer, tenants skip rent, municipalities issue sudden repair mandates. Reserves are your safety net. Without them, the smallest shock can send even a healthy deal into freefall.

Jane's Lesson in Reserve Discipline

Rossi Monroe brought up reserves during Jane's review of the Texas property. Jane's underwriting showed three months of operating expenses set aside at acquisition.

"Three months?" Rossi asked, leaning forward.

"That's what the investment offering showed," Jane said.

Rossi shook her head. "If everything goes perfectly, that might last you three months. But we do not underwrite for perfection. We underwrite for reality."

Jane learned that reserves are not about maximizing efficiency — they are about maximizing survivability.

The Two Types of Reserves Every Investor Needs

1. Operating Expense Reserves (Opex Reserves)

Also called a *Rainy Day Fund* or *working capital fund*, these are funds set aside to cover ongoing operating costs in case of cash flow disruption.

Typical guidance:

- Conservative – 6 months of operating expenses *plus* 6 months of debt service.

- Moderate – 4–6 months of operating expenses *plus* 4–6 months of debt service.

- Minimum – 6 months of operating expenses only (only for low-risk markets and strong sponsor profiles).

Why it matters:

Operating reserves buy time. If occupancy dips, leasing takes longer, or rent collections slow, reserves allow you to continue paying staff, vendors, and lenders without defaulting.

In the Texas case, Rossi walked Jane through the formula:

- Operating expenses: $780,000 annually.

- Debt service: $540,000 annually.
- Six months of each = $660,000 total recommended Opex reserve at acquisition.

Jane's three-month reserve covered less than half that.

2. Capital Expenditure Reserves (CapEx Reserves)

These are earmarked for major repairs, replacements, or planned improvements — anything that is *not* routine maintenance.

Typical guidance:

- Validate the rehab scope with both a contractor and property manager.
- Add a 10–15% contingency (20% in high-cost or volatile markets).
- Never rely solely on lender-funded draws — you may have to pay contractors before draws are reimbursed.

Why it matters:

Construction almost never comes in under budget. Supply chain issues, labor shortages, and hidden damage can easily blow through initial estimates. Without a buffer, you may find yourself cutting corners or pausing projects mid-stream, both of which erode property performance.

The Lender's Perspective

As a former lender, *Rossi added*, I can tell you: banks and agencies love reserves — they reduce default risk. That is why some loan structures require upfront reserve escrows for taxes, insurance, and replacement reserves (often $250–$300 per unit annually).

But lender requirements are often the *minimum*, not the *ideal*. Smart operators set their own, higher thresholds.

Case Studies in Reserve Failure

From the field, here are examples that prove why reserves are a non-negotiable:

- The Capital Call Spiral – A sponsor underwrote for 2 months of Opex reserves. A temporary eviction ban resulted in large economic vacancy and cash flow evaporated. They had to raise emergency capital from investors, diluting returns and eroding trust.

- The Tariff Shock – A value-add project budgeted $12,000 per unit for renovations. Midway through, imported materials spiked in cost due to new tariffs. Without a 15% contingency, they ran out of funds with 30% of units unfinished.

- The "Free" Rehab Illusion – A lender agreed to fund 100% of a $2 million rehab through construction draws. But the first draw required proof of completed work — meaning the sponsor had to front nearly $500,000 to get started. Without liquid reserves, they delayed the project by six months.

Jane's Reserve Rebuild

Rossi had Jane redo her sample deal underwriting:

- Increase Opex reserves from $325,000 to $660,000.

- Add a 15% contingency to the $1.2 million renovation budget, bringing it to $1.38 million.

- Plan to raise these amounts upfront rather than "find them later."

This dropped projected returns slightly — but it turned a fragile deal into one that could survive shocks.

"Your investors will thank you when something goes wrong and you do not call them for more money," Rossi said.

Practical Reserve Guidelines for Your Underwriting

1. Always separate Opex and CapEx reserves — they serve different purposes.

2. Match reserves to property age and condition — older assets need bigger buffers.

3. Confirm lender requirements but set your own higher — aim for survivability, not just compliance.

4. Front-load reserves — raising capital later is harder and costlier.

5. Revisit annually — adjust reserves as market conditions and property performance change.

The Trade-Off Myth

One of the most common pushbacks I hear, said Rossi, is:*"If we raise more for reserves, returns will be lower."*

Technically true — on paper. But in reality, well-funded reserves lower risk, which increases investor confidence, which in turn improves your ability to raise capital for future deals. Reserves are not a drag on returns; they are insurance for them.

With income and expenses validated and reserves in place, you now know the property's true operational strength and its ability to weather storms. The next question is: how much debt should you place on it, and on what terms?

Debt can amplify returns — or magnify losses. In Step 4, Rossi will walk Jane through the nuances of loan structures, leverage, interest rates, and amortization so you can avoid the trap of overleveraging in the pursuit of short-term gains.

Step 4: Debt Structure and Leverage Considerations

Debt: The Double-Edged Sword in Multifamily Investing

Debt is one of the most powerful tools in real estate — it can multiply returns, expand your buying power, and allow you to scale your portfolio faster than relying on cash alone. But like any powerful tool, when misused it can do more harm than good.

In multifamily underwriting, debt is not just a financing mechanism. It is a risk amplifier. The wrong loan structure can turn a great property into a problem child. The right loan, chosen with your business plan and market conditions in mind, can provide both stability and flexibility.

As a former commercial lender, *Rossi added*, I have seen deals fail not because the property was bad, but because the financing was mismatched to the business plan. In some cases, the terms themselves created risks the sponsor could not manage — balloon payments due in a frozen lending market, floating rates with no cap, or leverage so high there was no margin for error.

Jane's First Look at Loan Terms

After building a bulletproof income and expense profile, and ensuring reserves were adequate, Jane expected Rossi Monroe to be relieved. Instead, Rossi opened a new tab in the underwriting model and said:

"Now we talk about the debt."

Jane looked at the sponsor's summary:

- Loan-to-Value (LTV): 75%.
- Interest Rate: Floating at SOFR + 3%.
- Interest-Only: 3 years.
- Amortization: 30 years thereafter.
- Term: 5 years.

Rossi tapped the table. "This is where we see if the financing helps or hurts the deal."

Key Components of Debt Structure

1. Leverage (Loan-to-Value or Loan-to-Cost)

Leverage determines how much of the purchase (or total project cost) is financed with debt versus equity.

Guidance:

- Conservative: 55–70% LTV.
- Aggressive: 75–80%+ LTV.

Risks of high leverage:

- Higher debt service, reducing cash flow.
- Less margin if NOI and property values drop.
- Greater risk of breaching lender covenants (like Debt Service Coverage Ratio).

Why it matters in underwriting:

The higher the leverage, the more fragile the deal becomes to even small performance shortfalls.

2. Interest Rate Type: Fixed vs. Floating

Fixed Rate – Offers payment stability; ideal in rising rate environments.

Floating Rate – Can be cheaper upfront but exposes you to rate volatility; requires strong reserves and rate caps (or another form of interest rate hedging).

Rossi's rule: *"If you take floating debt, budget for the worst-case rate environment, not the best."*

3. Interest-Only (IO) Periods

IO periods reduce debt service early on, improving cash flow during renovations or lease-ups. But they do not reduce principal.

Best use: For value-add projects where NOI growth will outpace the amortization start date.

Risk: If projected NOI growth does not materialize, the jump in payments after the IO period expires can shock cash flow.

4. Amortization Schedule

Standard multifamily loans often use a 25–30 year amortization. A shorter amortization increases debt paydown but reduces near-term cash flow.

For long-term holds, stable cash flow, and gradual principal paydown, a 30-year amortization is common in multifamily (other asset classes do not always enjoy this). For higher equity buildup and lower lifetime interest cost, a shorter schedule can be beneficial — if the cash flow supports it.

5. Loan Term and Maturity

Your loan term must match your business plan:

- Short-term bridge: 1–3 years (value-add, heavy reposition).
- Permanent loan: 5–10 years (stabilized assets).

Maturity risk is real — if your loan comes due during a soft market or high interest rate environment, refinancing may be costly or impossible without a capital infusion.

Lender Covenants and Ratios

Debt Service Coverage Ratio (DSCR)

DSCR = NOI ÷ Debt Service

- Lenders typically require at least 1.25x DSCR.

- Your underwriting should aim higher for safety — 1.40x+ at actuals.

Debt Yield

Debt Yield = NOI ÷ Loan Amount

- A lender risk measure; higher is safer.

- Many lenders require 8–10% minimum debt yield for stability.

Loan-to-Cost (LTC)

For construction or major renovation projects, LTC compares loan amount to total cost (purchase + rehab + soft costs).

Jane's Stress Test

Rossi walked Jane through the Texas deal:

- At the current floating rate, DSCR was a comfortable 1.35x in Year 1.

- But if SOFR rose by 2%, DSCR dropped to 1.05x — dangerously close to breaching covenants.

- With 75% LTV, a modest 10% drop in value could push the property underwater relative to the loan balance.

Jane adjusted the model:

- Reduced LTV to 68%.

- Swapped to a fixed rate for stability.

- Added an extra 6 months of debt service to reserves.

The deal's projected IRR dipped slightly, but its survival odds in a rising rate environment improved dramatically.

Practical Tips for Debt Underwriting

1. Match term to business plan — Never use short-term debt for a long-term hold unless you have a clear refinance or sale plan.

2. Stress-test rates — Model scenarios at +1%, +2%, and +3% above your starting rate.

3. Cap floating rate risk — If traditional fixed rate is not available, then buy an interest rate cap or another interest rate hedge instrument, and budget the cost.

4. Do not max leverage — High LTV is tempting but leaves no margin for error.

5. Keep DSCR headroom — Target 1.40x+ based on *actual* Year 1 numbers.

With debt structured to fit the business plan, you have the last major input for your financial model. But there is one more critical variable — the cap rate.

Cap rates influence both the value you are paying now and the value you can sell for later. In Step 5, Rossi will show Jane how small shifts in cap rates can multiply into huge valuation swings — and how to underwrite with a margin of safety instead of relying on a perfect market at exit.

Step 5: Cap Rate, Valuation, and Risk Adjustments

The Multiplier You Cannot Ignore

When most new investors think about property value, they picture a simple equation:

Value = Price someone is willing to pay.

In multifamily investing, valuation is far more mechanical — and the central gear is the **capitalization rate**, or **cap rate**.

Cap rates seem simple:

Cap Rate = NOI ÷ Purchase Price

But as Rossi Monroe told Jane during their sample deal review, *"This one little number is like a magnifying glass. Small changes in cap rate can make big changes in value — both good and bad."*

That is why Step 5 in the five-step underwriting blueprint is so important.

What a Cap Rate Really Means

At its core, the cap rate is the property's unleveraged return — the yield you would get if you bought the property in cash.

A **6% cap rate** means the property produces $60,000 in NOI for every $1 million in value.

But here is the nuance:

- A higher cap rate usually means higher perceived risk (older property, weaker market, uncertain income stability).

- A lower cap rate usually means lower perceived risk (newer property, strong market, stable tenants).

Cap Rate at Purchase vs. Cap Rate at Exit

Rossi explained it this way:

- **Market Cap Rate** – The cap rate at which properties are trading at currently.

- **Purchase Cap Rate** – Your starting point (= Actual TTM NOI / Purchase Price). Are you paying above or below market?

- **Exit Cap Rate** – Your *assumption* for what the market will be when you sell (= Exit TTM NOI/ Sale Price).

If you buy at a **5.5% cap** and sell at a **6.0% cap**, the property's value will drop even if NOI stays flat (as demonstrated in the various examples in Chapter 5 and further down below). Conversely, if the market compresses and you sell at a lower cap rate, your value will jump.

This is why underwriters often **assume cap rate expansion** (increase) between purchase (market cap rate) and sale (exit cap rate) — it is a conservative hedge against market softening.

Jane's Exit Cap Reality Check

The deal pro forma showed:

- Purchase Cap Rate: 6.0% (in line with current market).

- Exit Cap Rate (Year 5): 5.5%.

Jane frowned. "So they are assuming the market will get better in five years?"

"Exactly," Rossi said. "That is speculation, not underwriting. We need to model the opposite — a softer market, not a better one."

They adjusted the exit cap to 6.0%. That one change lowered the projected sales price by over $1.5 million — enough to cut IRR by more than two points.

The Sensitivity Problem

Cap rates act as a **valuation multiplier**. A small movement — 25 basis points — can have a large impact:

Example:

- NOI = $1,000,000

- Cap Rate = 5.50% → Value = $18,181,818

- Cap Rate = 5.75% → Value = $17,391,304

- Cap Rate = 6.00% → Value = $16,666,667

That 50 bps change from 5.5% to 6.0% drops value by ~$1.5 million without touching income or expenses.

Market-Based Cap Rate Analysis

When validating cap rates, use multiple sources:

- **CoStar, Real Capital Analytics, CBRE (or other brokerage) reports** – for historical and recent sales comps.

- **Broker opinion of value** – but cross-check for optimism bias.

- **Lender input** – they often have their own current market ranges.

- **Appraisal data** – from recent financings in your target submarket.

And remember: the market cap rate is an *average* — if your property has higher risk factors than the average, adjust upward.

Risk Adjustments in Valuation

Beyond cap rate shifts, other valuation adjustments can protect your underwriting from over-optimism:

1. **NOI Cushion** – Model a 5-10% drop in NOI and see if the deal still works.

2. **Exit Timing Flexibility** – Do not assume you can sell in Year 5 exactly; have a range.

3. **Cost of Sale** – Include broker commissions, closing costs, and transfer taxes (and loan prepayment penalties, if applicable).

4. **Refinance Stress Test** – If you plan to refinance, test proceeds against higher rates and higher exit caps.

Jane's Final Risk Model

By adjusting the Texas deal's exit cap from 5.5% to 6.0%, adding a 5% NOI drop scenario, and including 2% in selling costs, Jane saw the IRR compress from 16% to 11%.

"It is not as exciting," she said.

"It is more real," Rossi replied. "Better to be surprised on the upside than blindsided on the downside."

Practical Tips for Cap Rate & Valuation Underwriting

1. **Be conservative at exit** – 10 bps higher (for each year of holding the property) than the entry market cap rate.

2. **Know your market's history** – Some markets swing more than others.

3. **Model multiple scenarios** – Best case, base case, and worst case.

4. **Do not anchor to broker pricing** – It is a starting point, not gospel.

Bringing It All Together

By now, Jane has validated income, expenses, reserves, debt, and valuation assumptions. The last step is to bring them together into a single decision — a red flag review that weighs the deal as a whole.

With the five steps now detailed and defined, Rossi then guided Jane through a complete walk-through of the deal using all five steps — demonstrating how a deal that looked promising in an investment deck can unravel under disciplined underwriting.

Bringing It All Together: Final Decision-Making and Red Flag Review

Coming Full Circle

In the first chapter, Jane saw the property's name in bold type in a foreclosure notice. The deal she had proudly invested in three years earlier was being taken back by the lender. Her initial reaction was a swirl of disbelief, embarrassment, and confusion.

Now, armed with the five-step underwriting framework Rossi Monroe has drilled into her, Jane is back at the table — this time with the deal's original financials, the offering memorandum, and her own updated underwriting template.

Her goal: to see the Houston deal not as a failure, but as a lesson.

Step 1: Income Analysis – Overstated Rent Potential

At the time of investment, Jane had accepted the sponsor's claim that "market rents" were $150 higher than in-place rents. She remembered nodding at the sleek comp table, believing this was a conservative number.

With her new process, she saw the truth:

- Broker comps were 2–3 miles away in a better school district.

- Two comps were brand-new Class A builds — irrelevant for a 1980s Class C asset.

- All but one were offering "two months free" or similar concessions, which had not been factored in.

Had she adjusted for these, the actual rent gap would have been $35 — not enough to justify the projected NOI lift.

Missed red flag: Reliance on sponsor-provided comps without independent verification.

Step 2: Expense Validation – Unrealistic Operating Costs

The pro forma had shown an Operating Expense Ratio (OER) of 37%. Jane had thought nothing of it.

Now, she knew:

- Market norms for similar properties were 45–48%.

- Repairs & Maintenance were listed at $350/unit/year — well below the $500/unit floor for the age of the asset.

- Payroll was missing a leasing agent's salary because the seller self-managed.

- Insurance premiums were based on an outdated quote, before regional rate spikes.

When she normalized expenses, the property's Year 1 NOI dropped by $180,000 — erasing most of the cash flow cushion.

Missed red flag: Accepting below-market expenses without understanding they would rise to reality.

Step 3: Reserve Analysis – No Safety Net

The deal had raised only 2 months of operating reserves and no CapEx contingency beyond the initial renovation budget.

When a major HVAC system failed and insurance premiums jumped mid-renovation, the sponsor had to choose between delaying upgrades and requesting a capital call. To mask the underlying issue, they did not do a capital call but instead stopped executing on the business plan and the planned rehab.

Jane now calculated that:

- Six months of Opex reserves would have required an extra $500,000 at closing.

- A 15% CapEx contingency would have prevented the need for a capital call entirely (or in this case the need to abandon the business plan and stop capex altogether).

Missed red flag: Underestimating the importance of reserves as a survival tool.

Step 4: Debt Structure – Leverage Without Cushion

The Houston deal had been financed at 80% LTV, with a floating interest rate, no interest rate cap purchased (i.e. interest rate risk was not hedged), and no clarity on extension options beyond the 3-year horizon.

At acquisition, DSCR was 1.30x — fine on paper. But when rates rose 200 bps, DSCR fell below 1.00x. With NOI already below projections, the property was on shaky ground.

Refinancing was impossible at the higher rates without injecting more equity — and with the value now below the loan balance, the sponsor had no viable exit.

Missed red flag: No stress-testing of floating rate risk or DSCR under rate increases.

Step 5: Cap Rate & Valuation – Optimism at the Exit

The sponsor had bought at a 5.0% cap and underwritten an exit at a 4.5% cap (because they were confident rates will decrease and because one market report forecasted it will, which forecast the sponsor had taken as the gospel).

Jane now saw the flaw:

- The market was already trending toward higher cap rates due to interest rate hikes.

- A conservative underwrite would have modeled an exit at 6.0% (in a rising interest rate environment).

- That alone would have lowered projected IRR by 3–4%, signaling the deal was too thin to absorb additional risks.

Missed red flag: Assuming market improvement at exit instead of allowing for softening.

The Post-Mortem Summary

Jane's re-underwrite of the Houston deal was sobering:

Category	Sponsor Projection	Jane's Revised
Rent Gap	+$150/unit	+$35/unit
OER	37%	47%
Reserves	2 months Opex	6 months Opex + 15% CapEx contingency
LTV	80%	60-70% safer
Exit Cap	4.5%	6.0%
Projected IRR	20%	<8%

Looking at the numbers side-by-side, she realized something powerful:

> "It was never really a 20%+ IRR deal. It was a high-risk bet disguised as a stable investment."

When she further examined the quarterly financials from her now stale portal, she noticed:

- Actual rents and NOI that never materialized relative to the original projections (the prior deals her friends had so fondly spoken of at the BBQ get together had been "bailed out" by cap rate compression).

- As the rents were declining and vacancy increasing, cash flow started deteriorating and cash balances were being depleted quickly.

- The projected exit cap rate compression only created an outcome that turned out to be a beautiful mirage far from reality.

- The writing had been on the wall all along…if only had she paid attention beyond the "deal is going ok" verbiage.

From Loss to Leverage (of a Different Kind)

The Houston foreclosure cost Jane both money and confidence. But dissecting it with Rossi's guidance turned the loss into a masterclass.

She saw, in black and white, how applying each of the five steps would have flagged the risks before she wired a single dollar. And she understood something else — that disciplined underwriting is not about killing deals. It is about finding the ones worth your capital.

Reflection space: If you have ever felt that knot in your stomach when a deal underperforms, you know the importance of what Jane just did. This framework is your safeguard. Use it, question everything, and remember: the best investment you will ever make is in your own due diligence.

As Rossi told Jane when they closed the binder on the Houston review:

> "Deals will come and go. Your capital, once lost, may not come back. But the skill to protect it? That stays with you forever."

CHAPTER 7

ADVANCED TIPS AND STRATEGIC INSIGHTS

Quick Valuation Checks for Initial Screening

Why Quick Screening Matters

Rossi liked to remind Jane that underwriting is not only about mastering the numbers but also about mastering *time*. A full, line-by-line financial model can take hours. Multiply that by a dozen deals in your inbox and you quickly find yourself buried.

"This is why you need a first filter," Rossi said one afternoon, as she pulled up a new offering memorandum. "A quick valuation check is like a metal detector at the airport. If it does not pass here, you do not even need to open your bag."

For a busy investor, these early checks are not a shortcut to avoid due diligence. They are a discipline that keeps you from chasing poor deals down a rabbit hole. They help you decide—quickly and confidently—whether to commit more time for deep due diligence or move on.

The Concept: A Two-Stage Underwriting Process

Underwriting works best when it is approached in two stages:

1. **Initial Screening** – The *go/no-go* stage where you determine whether the deal has a realistic chance of meeting your investment criteria.

2. **Full Underwrite** – The deep dive that tests every assumption, runs scenarios, and validates all the numbers.

The focus here is on Stage 1. Done right, you should be able to run this process in 15–30 minutes per deal.

Think of it as the "triage" stage: you are not diagnosing the entire patient—you are deciding who gets admitted for further examination.

Core Quick Valuation Checks

1. Purchase Price vs. Market Reality

Start with the most basic but most telling question: is the purchase price in line with the market?

- **Cap Rate Comparison** – Compare the going-in cap rate to current market averages for similar property class and location. If the offering is at a noticeable premium (say, a 4.5% cap in a 6% cap market) without a compelling, evidence-based reason, it should raise concerns.

- **Price Per Door** – Benchmark against recent sales in the submarket. A 20% deviation without explanation should prompt caution. Furthermore, if the price per door is higher than the median home price, that is a warning flag as it indicates it might be cheaper to own vs. rent in that sub-market. Lastly, if the price per door is above replacement cost, it indicates that it is cheaper to build that unit brand new vs. buy existing at the higher price point (thereby indicating potential over valuation).

Insider Warning: Numbers can be massaged to justify almost any price. Your job is to anchor valuation to objective, verifiable market data.

2. Rent Assumption Reality Check

A deal can look great on paper if you simply stretch the rent growth line. That is why one of your first checks is to verify in-place rents and the plausibility of projected increases.

- **Current Rent Verification** – Cross-reference with third-party data (CoStar, Apartments.com, Rent. com) or a quick call to the property pretending to be a prospective tenant.

- **Planned Rent Lifts** – If the plan calls for $300/ unit increases in a market where $100–$150 is the norm, you need proof—comparable renovated units, documented demand, and rent rolls. Conversely, if the rent lift is $50 or less, it raises the question on what the real upside is with the deal (especially with rehab involved, the project ROI needs to be present).

- **Stabilization Period** – Unrealistic speed is a common pitfall. A property with 40 units to renovate should not show "fully stabilized" in three months.

3. Day-One Cash Flow

If your investment criteria include positive cash flow from Day One, this check is non-negotiable (especially if you are a cash flow investor; if you invest solely for yield, that criterion would not apply).

- **Calculate:** NOI – Debt Service – Asset Management Fees. Is the end result a positive or a negative number?

- If the result is negative for multiple years, ask yourself if you are prepared to take on that risk and whether the projected rent growth justifies it.

- One indicator for cash flow is **positive leverage** (defined in Chapter 5). If the deal is purchased at negative leverage, it will most likely not cash flow on Day 1. In that case, if you do decide to move forward, it is imperative to understand the value-add upside and how realistic it is.

- Another indicator for cash flow is **the 1% rule**. If the annual rental income is less than 1% of the purchase price per door, it is unlikely the property will cash flow. While this is a rule of thumb from the single-family home space, for multifamily it is directional and not absolute.

4. Market Health Snapshot

As discussed in detail in Chapter 4, a property can be perfectly priced and still be a poor investment if the market fundamentals are weak.

At the initial screen stage, you should be able to at a minimum quickly gather:

- Median Household Income (preferably ≥ $50K).

- **Population Growth Trends.**

- **Job Base and Diversity** – Avoid single-employer towns.

- **Crime Data** – Especially for violent crime rates in the immediate area.

Case Example: A "close to a major MSA" deal turned out to be in a Class C– area with declining population and limited employment diversity. Proximity to a large city could not offset the local market's structural weaknesses.

5. Qualitative Criteria

Often one may rule out a property because it does not fit certain qualitative criteria such as: location, neighborhood, unit count (too small for your liking), unit mix (all one-bedroom units), property age (e.g., 1960s), or mechanicals (e.g., aluminum wiring, Zinsco electrical panels, well and septic tank presence, etc.).

Lastly, while this book focuses on the underwriting aspect of vetting a deal, vetting the operator/lead sponsor/ fund manager, is even more important, as execution is key. For additional resources on vetting the operator, access the free resources that come with the book here: www. MasteringMultifamilyUnderwriting.com/book-resources.

How Jane Learned to Use Quick Checks

At first, Jane wanted to deep-dive into every deal that came across her desk. "But I feel like I'm missing opportunities if I don't model everything!" Rossi stopped her.

"You are wasting your sharpest analysis on deals that fail the first filter," she said. "If the water in the well is bad, you do not need to test every bucket."

Rossi taught Jane to:

1. Pull the investment offering and skim to the property overview, market overview, and financial summary.

2. Run the five checks above in under 30 minutes.

3. Only move forward if at least four out of five pass the "sanity" threshold.

Within a few weeks, Jane could screen deals with the same speed and accuracy Rossi used—freeing her to focus on truly viable opportunities.

Exercise: Your First Quick Check

Pick an offering currently in your inbox. Without opening a full underwriting model:

1. Compare the purchase price cap rate and price per door to market.

2. Verify in-place rents and compare to pro forma projections.

3. Is the deal with positive leverage (assuming the package shared the all-in interest rate on the loan)?

4. Calculate day-one cash flow.

5. Pull basic market stats: median income, job diversity, crime rates.

Decide: does this deal deserve your next 5–10 hours? If yes, move it to the "deep analysis" pile. If not, archive it and move on.

The Discipline of Saying "No" Early

One of the hardest skills for new investors is passing on a deal early, especially if it looks exciting in the offering. Quick valuation checks protect you from the "glossy deck effect"—falling in love with the presentation before confirming the fundamentals.

Jane's early mistakes were costly because she skipped this stage. Now, she trusts her process. She knows that every "no" is not a missed opportunity but a step toward the right one.

Quick screening is not about being cynical—it is about being selective. Your time is your most valuable asset. By filtering with discipline, you ensure that when you do go deep, it is on a deal that deserves your best thinking. And as Rossi reminded Jane, "The right deal will stand up to a quick check. If it crumbles in the first pass, you have just saved yourself time, money, and heartache."

Leveraging Technology and AI Tools in Underwriting

The Role of Technology in Modern Underwriting

In the early days, underwriting a multifamily deal was a purely manual process. Investors pulled data from multiple sources, keyed it into spreadsheets, and built macros and pro formas line by line. It was time-consuming—and error-prone.

Today, technology can compress what used to take hours into minutes. AI-powered platforms, subscription data services, and purpose-built underwriting models can help you move from the quick screening stage into a full analysis with greater speed and accuracy.

But Rossi cautioned Jane early on: "Technology is a scalpel, not a surgeon. You still need to guide the cut."

How Technology Fits into the Five-Step Blueprint

Every tool or platform should support one or more of your core underwriting steps:

1. **Income Analysis and Rent Comps** – AI can scrape rental listings, filter by unit size, and calculate average market rents instantly.

2. **Expense Validation** – Integrated market reports can compare your expense assumptions to industry benchmarks.

3. **Reserve Analysis** – Some models automate reserve calculations and flag when capital expenditure budgets are unrealistic.

4. **Debt Structure and Leverage Considerations** – Loan calculators and rate feeds can simulate debt service under different scenarios.

5. **Cap Rate, Valuation, and Risk Adjustments** – Data sets can pull recent sales to benchmark entry and exit cap rates.

Core Categories of Underwriting Tools

1. Pre-Built Underwriting Models

Many experienced investors start with established Excel templates designed for multifamily syndications.

- **The Syndicated Deal Analyzer** – The model is a popular one with beginners as it is simple, flexible, and designed for quick navigation between key assumptions (rents, expenses, debt, reserves).

- **Other Popular Templates** – As Rossi explained, some partners prefer their own custom models. The goal is not to force them into your template but to master your five-step blueprint so you can spot assumptions quickly in *any* model.

Insider Warning: Pre-built models are only as good as the data you put in. Always verify the source.

2. Market Data Platforms

Fast access to accurate market data is essential for rent and expense verification.

- **CoStar or Crexi** – Comprehensive data on rents, sales comps, vacancy rates, and market trends (including new construction).

- **Yardi Matrix or Real Page** – Deep data on property-level details, supply-demand and construction pipeline, and submarket performance.

- **Broker Reports** – provide quarterly data on various markets and asset classes (e.g. CBRE, Berkadia, Marcus & Millichap, Cushman & Wakefield, etc.).

3. AI-Powered Screening

Artificial intelligence can help process large volumes of deals and flag potential opportunities or risks.

- **AI Rent Scrapers** – Compare current rents to pro forma assumptions without manual calls.

- **AI Underwriting Software Programs** – can provide a preliminary underwrite in minutes. Examples include: Cash Flow Portal, Clik.ai, etc.

- **Document Review AI** – Extracts key pieces of information from the offering package or broker package. Examples include: Notebook LM, Chat GPT, Claude, Gemini, etc.

- **GPTs** – Designed to complete specific tasks like market analysis, prelim sponsor vetting, deal profile summary, etc. To access the market analysts GPT, go here: www.MasteringMultifamilyUnderwriting.com/book-resources.

Jane's First Technology Win

After mastering her quick valuation checks, Jane's next challenge was deal volume. She had more opportunities to review than she could manually handle. Rossi introduced her to the Market Vetting Assistant, the Sponsor Vetting Assistant, and the Deal Vetting Assistant GPTs (you can access all of them here: (www.MasteringMultifamilyUnderwriting.com/book-resources).

Within minutes, Jane could:

- Verify market KPIs.

- Do preliminary diligence on a sponsor.

- Run high level prelim deal analysis to highlight key gaps or red flags.

For Jane, the shift was not about replacing her judgment—it was about amplifying her capacity and efficiency.

Best Practices for Using Tech in Underwriting

1. **Validate Before Trusting** – Always test a new platform against a deal you have fully underwritten manually. See if the results match and where they differ. It is not uncommon for AI (at least at today's stage of development) to hallucinate and make mistakes. **Do not rely solely on AI when making 5-6-7+ figure financial decisions.**

2. **Keep Control of Assumptions** – Do not let software default settings dictate your pro forma inputs.

3. **Stay Current** – Market data ages quickly; update rent comps, expense benchmarks, and cap rates, regularly.

4. **Combine Tools** – No single platform will give you everything. Use a blend of market data, financial modeling, and AI validation.

5. **Maintain Your Skill** – Technology should complement—not replace—your ability to underwrite with pen, paper, and calculator if needed.

By now, you can screen deals quickly and enhance your accuracy with technology. But data and software are not your only allies. The next layer of underwriting insight comes from *people*—your network of fellow investors, brokers, lenders, and operators who can give you off-market intelligence no spreadsheet can match.

Building a Network for Off-Market Insights

Why Relationships Still Matter

After exploring quick screening and technology tools, Jane thought she finally had a complete system. But Rossi smiled knowingly. "Technology will show you the numbers. Your network will tell you the *story.*"

In multifamily investing, deals are rarely won purely on data. The best opportunities often never make it to public listing platforms, and the biggest risks are sometimes invisible in the financials. These are discovered through relationships—conversations with people who live and breathe the market every day.

The Two Types of Off-Market Intelligence

1. **Deal Flow Intel** – Opportunities not widely marketed or sent only to a select group of trusted investors.

2. **Market Reality Intel** – Local truths that do not appear in the OM (offering memo)—like a major employer planning layoff, or a proposed development that will flood the market with new units or a bad sponsor.

A strong network gives you both.

Who Belongs in Your Network

1. Brokers

- Primary source for new opportunities, especially if you have a track record of responding quickly and closing reliably.

- Value comes from being on their "first call" list when a deal is about to hit the market.

2. Property Managers

- Boots-on-the-ground knowledge of tenant profiles, rent collection realities, and operational challenges.

- Can flag discrepancies between marketed rents and actual achievable rents.

3. Lenders and Loan Brokers

- Know which deals are being financed, which are struggling to close, and the underwriting standards lenders are applying in real time.

4. Other Investors

- Peer networks, investor meetups, and online forums can reveal patterns in sponsor behavior, market trends, and hidden red flags.

How Network Intel Changes Decisions

Case Example:

A multifamily deal in a "growing" submarket passed the quick valuation and rent comp checks. But a local property manager mentioned the submarket had one dominant employer whose contract was up for renewal. The risk of mass layoffs was high. That deal never made it past Jane's initial interest—saving months of wasted effort and potential capital loss.

Case Example:

In another instance, an investor peer group flagged a sponsor who had gone through a number of capital calls and was still actively raising money for net new deals out there.

Building and Maintaining Your Network

1. **Start with Mutual Value** – Do not just collect contacts; contribute information, introductions, or other insights when possible.

2. **Be Consistent** – Regular touchpoints matter. A quarterly check-in call or market update email keeps you on people's radar.

3. **Attend Strategic Events** – Local multifamily meetups, regional real estate conferences, and virtual roundtables are efficient ways to expand your circle.

4. **Leverage Digital Platforms** – LinkedIn, investor online groups and forums, and niche forums can connect you with out-of-area market experts.

Jane's Network Breakthrough

Jane's first real win from networking came when Rossi introduced her to a veteran property manager in a market Jane had been watching. In a 20-minute call, she learned:

- Which neighborhoods had the strongest tenant demand.

- Which ones were plagued by high crime despite promising population stats.

- Which value-add plays were overdone and now saturated.

Armed with that information, Jane avoided chasing two deals that looked fine on paper but were doomed to underperform.

Combining Network Intel with Data and Tech

Your underwriting process becomes most powerful when these three elements work together:

- **Quick Valuation Checks** filter out obvious mismatches.

- **Technology & AI Tools** speed up data collection and verification.

- **Network Insights** fill in the story behind the numbers and reveal factors you cannot see in the spreadsheet.

This combination not only saves time but also builds conviction in your decisions.

Exercise: Relationship Map

Draw a simple map of your current multifamily network:

1. List your contacts in each category (brokers, property managers, lenders, investors).

2. Note the markets they cover, their area of expertise, and the quality of the relationship (1–5 scale).

3. Identify two gaps to fill in the next 90 days.

Set one tangible action per gap—such as attending a specific meetup, scheduling a call, or making a LinkedIn introduction request.

Numbers may form the skeleton of a deal, but your network gives it flesh and blood. The stronger your relationships, the more likely you are to spot opportunity early and avoid unseen danger. As Rossi told Jane, "Deals may live in spreadsheets, but the truth lives in conversations."

Next, we will look at how to keep your underwriting skills sharp, adapt to market shifts, and remain a step ahead of the competition.

Continuing Education and Staying Ahead of the Curve

Why Underwriting Is a Moving Target

The fundamentals of underwriting may be constant—income, expenses, reserves, debt, and valuation—but the *inputs* are in constant motion. Interest rates shift. Rent growth cools or accelerates. Operating costs fluctuate with insurance premiums, utility rates, and labor shortages.

Rossi reminded Jane, "You can learn the framework once, but you cannot freeze your knowledge. Underwriting is like a language—stop speaking it, and you will lose fluency."

The Cost of Standing Still

Markets reward adaptability. The investors who underwrote deals in 2021 using rosy rent growth assumptions learned this the hard way in 2023, when interest rates spiked and operating expenses surged.

Those who kept their skills fresh were the first to adjust:

- Slowing rent growth projections to match softening demand.

- Factoring in higher insurance and payroll costs.

- Stress testing at higher exit cap rates.

For Jane, this meant revisiting the same five-step blueprint she had mastered (detailed in Chapter 6), but with new data and updated market perspectives.

Core Habits for Staying Sharp

1. Regular Market Reviews

- Stay abreast of global and geopolitical events that inevitably impact capital markets.

- Keep current with macro and local market news and trends.

- Subscribe to various market and broker insights reports to get the latest news and trends.

2. Deal Practice

Even if you are not actively investing, continue underwriting real deals coming your way. Treat it like going to the gym: reps build muscle memory.

3. Post-Mortems

Analyze past deals you passed on or invested in:

- Did the property perform as underwritten?

- What assumptions were accurate, and which missed the mark?

- What signals did you overlook?

4. Learning from Peers

Join roundtables, webinars, or mastermind groups. Peer discussions often surface changes in lender sentiment, operator practices, and market behavior before they appear in the data.

Sources of Ongoing Learning

Several reliable channels can keep you current:

- **Industry Reports** – CBRE, Marcus & Millichap, and Berkadia issue quarterly reports that highlight macro trends.

- **Specialized Forums** – Online investor groups, property management boards, and real estate syndication communities.

- **Technology Updates** – As covered earlier, AI and data platforms evolve quickly; track new features that can improve speed or accuracy.

- **Conferences & Meetups** – Exposure to different markets, emerging strategies, and the latest underwriting tools.

Jane's Commitment to Lifelong Learning

After building her network, Jane began blocking time every month to refresh her underwriting skills. Some months, it was running through three new deals just to test assumptions. Other months, it was attending a lender webinar on evolving DSCR and loan structure requirements.

One year later, Jane's confidence was no longer just in her framework—it was in her ability to apply it in any market condition.

Balancing Technology and Human Insight

As AI tools advance, it can be tempting to outsource more of the process. But Rossi reminded Jane that technology is most valuable when paired with:

- **Her critical thinking skills** – to challenge assumptions.

- **Her network's local knowledge** – to validate data against lived reality.

- **Her experience** – to spot patterns software cannot yet recognize.

Exercise: Continuing Education Plan

1. **Identify Three Areas for Growth** – e.g., debt structuring, market analysis, or asset management metrics.

2. **Select One Action Per Area** – such as a specific course, conference, or subscription report.

3. **Schedule It** – Put it in your calendar now, not "someday."

4. **Review Quarterly** – Reassess whether your education is keeping pace with market changes.

Mastery is not a one-time achievement—it is a cycle of learning, applying, and refining. The investors who thrive long-term are those who treat underwriting as a living skill, not a static checklist.

As Rossi told Jane, "Deals change. Markets change. The only constant is your commitment to staying sharp."

With this chapter, you have completed the Advanced Tips and Strategic Insights section. You now have the tools to:

- Screen deals quickly.

- Leverage technology with discernment.

- Build a network that gives you an information edge.

- Keep your skills relevant as markets evolve.

In the next chapter, you will apply everything you have learned alongside Jane to evaluate key aspects as well as red flags and green flags of various deals.

CHAPTER 8

CASE STUDIES AND REAL-WORLD APPLICATIONS

Jane Becomes a Pro: Multiple Mini-Deal Analyses and Decisions

Coffee, Spreadsheets, and Clarity

It was early on a Saturday, and the scent of fresh coffee filled Jane's kitchen. Her laptop screen glowed with the first of four new offerings that had landed in her inbox this week. A year ago, she would have jumped to the returns page, scanned for IRR and cash-on-cash, and let excitement guide her.

Now she opened each deal with a different mindset — methodical, skeptical, and guided by the five-step underwriting framework Rossi Monroe had drilled into her.

This was no longer about *finding* a reason to invest. It was about *proving* that a deal deserved her capital.

Mini-Deal #1 — The "Up-and-Coming" Mirage

The first package came from a syndicator Jane had met at a conference, eager to present a "can't miss" 120-unit Class B property in a "rapidly improving" Charlotte submarket. The

227

glossy photos were paired with bold numbers: current asking rents at $1,900 per unit, with a pro forma showing a $300 lift in just two years.

Jane's cursor hovered over the rent roll. Before she touched a formula cell, she opened Apartments.com to see what tenants were actually paying in that zip code. The average came in closer to $1,900 — not even close to the $2,200 proforma — and many of those units had newer finishes than the subject property.

A deeper look revealed an expense ratio of 39% — low for the market and a red flag for potential understatement. And then came the clincher: a quick text to a trusted local investor contact. "That area has been 'up-and-coming' for over a decade," the manager said with a chuckle. "It just hasn't come up yet."

With income assumptions inflated and the business plan leaning on a rent lift that history did not support, Jane closed the file.

Lesson for the Reader: Broker or operator optimism can outpace market reality. Verify before you believe.

Mini-Deal #2 — The Thin Reserve Risk

The second opportunity was from a seasoned Houston sponsor, offering an 18% projected IRR over a five-year hold. The slide deck was polished, with rent comps that seemed to justify pushing Class A rates from a solid Class B property.

Jane flipped to the reserves section and her eyebrows lifted. Only three months of operating expenses. In her training with Rossi, that number had always been a clear vulnerability — especially in a shifting market.

The pro forma included no stabilization period; rent increases began from day one. And the cap rate story was just as fragile: entry was already aggressive, and the exit assumed flat pricing despite signs the market was softening.

Jane adjusted the model with a more conservative lease-up period, a 25-basis-point cap rate expansion, and a reserve level matching six months of expenses. The IRR crumpled.

She closed the file without hesitation.

Lesson for the Reader: Even strong IRR projections collapse if reserves and assumptions are brittle.

Mini-Deal #3 — The Single-Employer Town

The third offering was a 75-unit property "just outside" a major metropolitan area, or so the OM claimed. The deck highlighted its proximity to the city but was quiet about the town's actual employment base.

Jane's market check quickly uncovered the truth: more than 60% of jobs came from a single manufacturing plant. She pulled crime data for the census tract and found violent crime rates significantly above metro averages.

She ran a quick scenario in her head. If the plant downsized — a not-uncommon event in towns dependent on one employer — tenant demand could collapse overnight.

For Jane, the decision was simple.

Lesson for the Reader: Job diversity is a pillar of market stability. If one employer's fortunes dictate the local economy, your deal is only as strong as that employer's next earnings report.

Mini-Deal #4 — The Quiet Winner

The last file of the morning came from a sponsor Jane had worked with before (a former co-worker turned full time real estate investor). It was a 90-unit property in a stable, mid-tier submarket. No flashy photos, no dramatic "transformational" plan. Just clean operations, steady occupancy, and metrics that fell neatly within her buy box.

The entry cap rate was 50 basis points above the market average — rare in current conditions. Rents were about $100 per unit below market, supported by clear and relevant comps. The business plan targeted that lift within 18 months.

Reserves? Six months of operating expenses plus a $500,000 CapEx contingency.

Jane felt herself nodding as she worked through the checklist. This was the kind of deal that might be overlooked by investors chasing excitement. But she knew better now.

This one went into her "deep dive" file for full underwriting.

Lesson for the Reader: The best deals are often the least flashy. Stability, realism, and conservative buffers beat showmanship every time.

Jane's Quick-Check Process

For the reader, Jane's journey through these four deals mirrors the same process you can follow when screening opportunities:

1. **Verify Income Claims** — Cross-check pro forma rents with live market data and honest comps.

2. **Test Expense Assumptions** — Compare to market norms; anything unusually low may be understated.

3. **Assess Market Fundamentals** — Look for job diversity, wage growth, and crime trends.

4. **Scrutinize Reserves** — Anything under six months of operating expenses invites risk.

5. **Identify Execution Risk** — Aggressive timelines or premium rent targets require proof, not hope.

Jane shut her laptop and poured herself a second cup of coffee. Three out of four deals had been easy passes — not because they lacked potential on paper, but because her process had stripped away the gloss.

The one deal that made it through was not the loudest or most glamorous. It was the one that respected the fundamentals.

She smiled. This was the real transformation: she no longer measured her success by how many deals she said "yes" to, but by the clarity and discipline in every "no."

One of the next deals on her list had a backstory that reminded her of Rossi's capital call warning — and she knew it deserved a deeper look. That would be her focus next.

Practice Exercise: Pull your last three investment opportunities (or find three current listings). Apply Jane's five-step screening process to each one. How many would have passed your initial filter? Document your findings - this will help you calibrate your screening criteria.

A Capital Call Case Study: Spotting the Warning Signs

The Message

The text came late on a Tuesday night.

Hi Jane, I know this is last minute… but could you look at something for me? My sponsor just called a capital call, and I am not sure what to do.

Jane's first thought was how familiar the situation felt. A year ago, she would have been the one sending this kind of message — anxious, under time pressure, and unsure what questions to ask.

Now she was on the other side.

Context — A Race Against the Clock

The investor, Michael, had put $100,000 into a multifamily deal eighteen months earlier. It had been marketed as a conservative value-add play in a strong market. Cash flow had been slow to materialize, but the sponsor assured everyone it was "within plan."

Then came the email:

We regret to inform you…

The message explained that without an immediate infusion of capital, the property risked default. Investors were asked to contribute their pro-rata share to cover "urgent operational needs" — within ten days.

Michael felt cornered. If he did not participate, his original capital could be lost. If he did, he was wiring in more money without knowing whether it would make a difference.

That is when he reached out to Jane.

From Student to Teacher

Jane opened the deal documents Michael forwarded. Her old self might have scanned the sponsor's narrative for reassurance. The Jane of today went straight to the numbers.

Step one was understanding exactly where the new money would go. Buried deep in the supplemental disclosure was a line item that stopped her cold: a significant portion of the capital call would be used to repay a shareholder loan owed to the lead sponsor.

She remembered Rossi's voice in her head: *Follow the money, and you will find the truth.*

Deep Dive — The Red Flags

Jane laid out her review for Michael, step by step:

1. **Exit Cap Rate Assumptions** — The underwriting assumed cap rate compression at exit — a 25-basis-point drop — despite today's softer market. When she adjusted to even a flat exit cap, projected IRRs and the exit valuation fell sharply.

2. **Rent Growth Projections** — The sponsor's Year 2 rent increases were pegged at 3% in a market where rents had declined in the past twelve months.

3. **Use of Funds** — Repaying the sponsor's own shareholder loan during a crisis was a conflict of interest not clearly highlighted in the original capital call notice.

4. **Risk Scenarios** — Under conservative rent growth and a flat or expanded exit cap, Michael would either lose his original capital now (if he did not participate) or later (if he did). The probability of a true turnaround was low without an extraordinary market rebound.

Jane knew these were the same patterns Rossi had warned her about back when she was still learning — overly rosy assumptions baked into the original underwriting, sponsors protecting their position first, and investors feeling trapped by urgency.

The Decision — Clarity Over Pressure

They spoke for thirty minutes. Jane explained the numbers, the sensitivities, and what it meant for his downside risk.

Michael exhaled audibly. "So, you are saying if I put in more money, I am likely just delaying the loss?"

"That is what the numbers are telling us," Jane said. "You have to decide whether that's a risk you are willing to take. But at least now, it is an informed choice."

Michael chose not to contribute to the capital call. It was not an easy decision, but it was one he made without the fog of sponsor pressure.

How to Evaluate a Capital Call

Jane's review process for Michael can serve as a checklist for any investor faced with a capital call:

- **Ask for a full breakdown of use of funds** — Be clear on whether the money will fix an operational problem, service debt, or repay insiders.

- **Compare actual performance to the original proforma (this will give you a good idea of the sponsor's history of meeting projections and how far apart they are) and re-run the revised projections presented with the capital call as if you are evaluating a brand-new investment** — Test the exit cap, rent growth, and expense assumptions against current market data.

- **Run downside scenarios** — Look at both "participate" and "do not participate" cases.

- **Identify conflicts of interest** — Is management benefiting directly from the new capital before the property stabilizes (e.g., full repayment of shareholder loans they made to the property or any additional fees assessed)?

- **Consider alternative outcomes** — Sometimes walking away sooner preserves capital for better opportunities later.

A Quiet Realization

After they hung up, Jane sat for a moment in the stillness of her kitchen.

She realized this was the first time she had been the one providing the clarity — not receiving it. A year ago, she had been Michael, hoping someone else would tell her what to do. Now, she could explain the numbers, frame the risks, and give someone the confidence to make their own call.

It was not just about underwriting anymore. It was about becoming the kind of investor who could stand steady when the pressure hit.

In the days that followed, Michael emailed her to say thank you. "That was the best thirty minutes I have spent on an investment decision," he wrote.

Jane smiled when she read it. She had not saved his capital — the loss was still real — but she had helped him avoid throwing more money after it.

This was what Rossi meant when she talked about *returning with the elixir*. Knowledge, applied at the right moment, can be the most valuable asset an investor has.

And Jane knew she would carry this clarity into every deal she touched from here on.

Prepare for the Unexpected: Create your own capital call evaluation checklist based on Jane's framework. Save this template where you can access it quickly if you ever receive that late-night capital call request. Being prepared reduces emotional decision-making.

The Deal That Didn't Add Up

A Promising Start

The email came from a syndicator Jane had met at a networking event a few months earlier.

"Jane, I think you'll love this one. Strong returns, heavy value-add, proven sponsor."

Attached was a crisp offering for a 220-unit property in a growing Southern metro. The headline numbers were hard to ignore: projected IRR of 20%, cash-on-cash in the double digits by year three, and a sleek renovation plan that promised to "reposition the asset to Class A standards."

Jane poured a fresh cup of coffee and opened the file. This was the kind of deal she would have jumped at two years ago. Now, she knew better.

The Business Plan

The sponsor's strategy was ambitious:

- Renovate every unit with high-end finishes.

- Add amenities like a fitness center and co-working space.

- Push rents well above current market averages.

- Stabilize in twelve months.

On paper, the transformation looked impressive. But Jane had learned from Rossi that complexity in a business plan is not the same as strength. "The more moving parts," Rossi used to say, "the more ways things can go wrong."

Peeling Back the Layers

Jane's first step was to compare the pro forma rent growth to actual market history. The sponsor projected an 8% rent lift in year one, followed by steady 3% annual growth.

A quick check in CoStar told a different story: the submarket's average rent growth over the last five years hovered around 1.5% — and last year had actually been negative.

Next, she looked at the stabilization timeline. Twelve months to renovate 220 units and achieve full lease-up was aggressive by any standard. Jane modeled a more realistic twenty-four-month period.

Finally, she examined the fee structure. On the surface, it looked standard: acquisition fee, asset management fee, construction management fee. But a deeper read revealed layering — the GP would collect fees on top of fees, plus there was a preferred equity tranche that took priority over limited partner distributions.

That meant much of the LP capital raised up front would be used to service the preferred equity partner's interest payments — before Jane or any other LP saw a dime.

The Turning Point — Numbers Don't Lie

With just three adjustments — realistic rent growth, extended stabilization, and the impact of fees — the model told a new story.

Projected profit became a net loss by the end of the hold period. Cash flow in the early years turned negative. The shiny IRR dropped into the single digits, far below Jane's minimum threshold.

She stared at the spreadsheet. Two hours ago, this had been a deal worth getting excited about. Now it was clear: the margin for error was razor thin, and the assumptions holding it together were more hopeful than probable.

The Conversation

Jane called the sponsor. "I have some concerns about your rent growth projections and the stabilization timeline," she began.

There was a pause. "We're confident we can hit those numbers," the sponsor replied. "We've done it before."

Jane asked for specifics — examples from the same market, with similar property size and scope. None were forthcoming.

That was all she needed to know.

Three Checks to Save Your Capital

For the reader, Jane's process here can serve as a simple filter before committing to a full investment:

1. **Market Reality vs. Pro Forma Optimism** – Always compare projected rent growth to historical data. If the story relies on an unprecedented jump, question it.

2. **Execution Timeline** – Aggressive stabilization schedules often underestimate the disruption of renovations and lease-up. Build in buffer.

3. **Fee Impact** – Fees layered on fees can drain investor returns. Understand not just the amount, but the sequence in which they are paid.

The Best Money You Never Lose

Jane passed on the deal. She sent the syndicator a polite note thanking them for the opportunity, but she knew in her gut — and in her spreadsheet — that this was a "no."

That night, she thought about Rossi's lesson: *Sometimes the best investment you can make is the one you do not make.*

And as she closed her laptop, Jane realized something else — she no longer needed permission to trust her own analysis. The numbers, once intimidating, were now her clearest guide.

Red Flag Training: Practice identifying over-optimistic assumptions. Take any current deal you are considering and intentionally stress-test three key assumptions: rent growth, stabilization timeline, and fees. This exercise builds your skepticism muscle.

A Successful Turnaround: The Right Operator, the Right Plan

A Familiar Name

The deal came from an operator Jane had followed for over a year but had never invested with. She had watched them present at conferences, read their quarterly letters, and noted how their past projects consistently hit or exceeded projections — even in challenging markets.

The email subject line read:

"Off-Market Opportunity — 180-Unit Value-Add, Proven Execution Team"

Jane clicked it open.

A Property with History

The property was a 1980s garden-style complex in a mid-sized, economically diverse city. Occupancy was solid at 93%, but rents lagged the market by about $125 per unit.

The backstory was intriguing — the seller had owned it for nearly twenty years, with minimal upgrades beyond basic maintenance. Curb appeal was decent, but interiors were dated.

The operator's plan was clear and focused:

- Renovate 60% of units with modern finishes.

- Add washer/dryer hookups to 50 units where plumbing allowed.

- Refresh landscaping and common areas.

- Implement professional management with a track record in the submarket.

No sweeping "Class A repositioning." No assumptions about pushing rents to luxury levels.

The Deep Dive — Testing the Numbers

Jane started with market rents. CoStar and Apartments.com all told the same story: renovated properties in the immediate area were achieving $120–$150 more per unit than the subject property's current rates.

Her next check was expenses. The pro forma assumed an expense ratio of 48% — in line with both her personal benchmarks and market norms. Maintenance and turnover budgets were realistic, with $500 per door allocated for repairs and $300 for turns.

Reserves stood at six months of operating expenses plus a 12% CapEx buffer — a sign the operator had thought about contingencies.

She then ran sensitivity tests:

- If rent lift came in at $100 instead of $125, IRR dropped from 15% to 13.4% — still acceptable.

- If renovations ran 10% over budget, returns held at just under 14%.

This was a deal with margin for error — the kind she rarely saw in recent years.

The Operator Factor

Numbers aside, Jane placed significant weight on who was running the deal.

This operator had:

- Completed six similar projects in the same metro, all profitable.

- Longstanding relationships with local contractors and suppliers.

- Transparent investor communications, including quarterly financials with actual vs. projected performance.

Jane called a past investor for reference. "They under promise and overdeliver," he said. "They don't win every battle, but they win the war."

Why This One Worked

Jane's "yes" decision was not about perfect projections. It was about:

1. **Realistic Business Plan** — Moderate, supported rent lifts with achievable timelines.

2. **Market-Aligned Expenses** — Benchmarks matched historical data, not wishful thinking.

3. **Adequate Reserves** — Enough cushion to handle the inevitable surprises.

4. **Proven Operator Execution** — A documented history of delivering in the same market.

5. **Resilient Returns** — Even in downside scenarios, the deal met her minimum thresholds.

Saying Yes with Confidence

Jane wired her funds two weeks later. She knew the deal would still require careful execution, but she felt aligned with both the numbers and the people running it.

When Rossi called to check in, Jane shared the details. There was a pause, and then Rossi laughed softly.

"You sound like you've been doing this for decades," she said.

Jane smiled. "I just learned from the best."

For her, this was more than an investment. It was proof that discipline could lead not only to smart "no's" but also to confident, calculated "yes's" — the kind that build wealth and peace of mind over time.

CHAPTER 9 [BONUS CHAPTER 1]

HOW LENDERS THINK — AND THE QUESTIONS TO ASK

Lender Priorities vs. Investor Priorities

Understanding the Different Lenses on the Same Deal

When a multifamily property goes through underwriting, it is tempting to assume that the lender's approval is a seal of safety for the investor. After all, if a bank or an agency lender is willing to put millions into a deal, they must have seen something solid.

That assumption can be dangerous. Lender underwriting and investor underwriting often overlap in certain ways, but the priorities, decision triggers, and tolerance for risk are not identical. A lender's main goal is straightforward: **get their money back, with interest, on time.** An investor's main goal is more nuanced: **earn a return that justifies the risk while preserving capital**.

The difference between these two goals can lead to decisions that feel perfectly reasonable to a lender but fall short for an investor — and vice versa.

The Lender's Primary Focus: Debt Repayment Above All

From years in commercial lending, I can tell you that a lender's thought process is not mysterious, but it is highly disciplined. Lenders approach every deal with one core filter: *Will this property generate enough stable cash flow, under conservative assumptions, to pay the debt as agreed for the entire loan term?*

The path to that answer involves several key priorities:

1. The Borrower's Strength

- Experience, track record, and operational competence are heavily weighted.

- Net worth and liquidity are measured against loan size (e.g., liquidity equal to at least 10% of loan amount, net worth equal to the loan amount itself).

- For syndicated deals, lenders may require general partners to contribute a minimum equity stake (often 10%+).

2. The Asset Itself

- Location quality, property condition, tenant profile, and market stability.

- The physical collateral must be solid enough to hold value and remain marketable even in a downturn.

3. Conservative Financial Stress Tests

- Lenders will size the loan not just on current performance, but on downside scenarios.

- This means adjusting pro forma numbers to reflect slower rent growth, higher expenses, or temporary vacancy.

4. Loan Structure and Covenants

- Terms such as debt service coverage ratio (DSCR) minimums, debt yield requirements, and negative covenants (e.g., restrictions on distributions, changes in management, or additional borrowing).

- Regular reporting requirements, from rent rolls to insurance certificates, are baked in to monitor ongoing compliance.

5. No Surprises

- Open communication is non-negotiable. Surprises, especially negative ones, erode trust and can trigger closer scrutiny or tightened terms.

The Investor's Primary Focus: Returns and Wealth Building

Investors look at the same property but through a different lens: *Will this investment generate acceptable returns for the level of risk, while preserving my principal?*

This shifts the emphasis to:

1. Projected Cash Flow and Total Return

- Cash-on-cash returns, internal rate of return (IRR), and equity multiple.

- Distribution timelines and the stability of projected payments.

2. Equity Growth Potential

- Value-add upside, rent growth assumptions, and capital appreciation over the hold period.

3. Capital Preservation

- Avoiding scenarios that could lead to capital calls, reduced distributions, or partial/full loss of principal.

4. Operator Alignment

- Fair fee structures and co-investment from the general partner.

- Business plan feasibility and operator's historical performance.

5. Exit Strategy

- Realism of the planned exit cap rate.

- Market conditions likely to prevail at the time of sale or refinance.

Where Lenders and Investors Overlap — and Where They Diverge

There is meaningful common ground. Both lenders and investors care about:

- The property's ability to produce steady income.

- The track record and reputation of the operator.

- Market fundamentals like job growth, household income, and supply-demand balance.

- And last but certainly not least, preservation of principal.

However, the divergence is where the risk lies for the investor:

Lenders prioritize downside protection. They focus on worst-case scenarios and how those impact debt repayment.

Investors often prioritize upside potential. While downside protection matters, it sometimes takes a back seat to projected returns.

An investor might approve a deal with minimal Year 1 cash flow because they are satisfied with the overall proforma returns and that DSCR covenants will be met from Year 2 onward. A lender, however, might find this unacceptable (unless they are a bridge lender, in which case positive cash flow is less of a factor).

Why a Lender's "Yes" Is Not an Investor's Green Light

It is important to remember: lender underwriting is a *credit* decision, not an *investment* decision.

A property can pass a lender's review because it meets conservative repayment criteria, yet still delivers mediocre or even negative returns for equity investors. The reality is that there are numerous lenders out there (not just banks and agencies, but also non-financial institutions), each with varying risk appetites and lending guidelines.

For example:

- **Thin Reserves:** A lender might accept a deal with six months of operating reserves because their main concern is whether debt payments are covered. An investor may want twelve months or more to cushion distributions during operational hiccups.

- **Aggressive Rent Growth Assumptions:** A lender might discount overly optimistic projections but still proceed if base-case income covers debt (they underwrite and size the loan based on actuals and not projections). Investors relying on that rent growth for return targets could be disappointed.

- **High Leverage with Strong Collateral:** A lender might feel comfortable at a higher loan-to-value ratio if the property is in a prime market, cash flows well, and the borrower is strong. For the investor, higher leverage means thinner margins for error.

How to Apply the Lender's Discipline to Your Own Analysis

Even though priorities differ, there is a valuable takeaway: investors can improve their decision-making by borrowing certain lender habits.

1. Stress Test Your Numbers

Run base-case and downside-case projections. What happens if rents grow slower, expenses run higher, or occupancy dips?

2. Focus on Covenants as Clues

Lender-imposed covenants reveal what they view as the deal's weak points. If there is a DSCR covenant at 1.35x instead of the more common 1.25x, that is a sign of perceived higher risk.

3. Evaluate the Borrower as a Business Partner

Just as lenders vet the borrower's net worth, liquidity, and track record, investors should vet the general partner with the same rigor.

4. Look Beyond Interest Rate and Amortization

Debt yield, negative covenants, and reporting requirements can signal potential challenges later.

A Quick Analogy: Seatbelt vs. Steering Wheel

Think of a lender as the seatbelt in a car. Their role is to ensure that if the ride gets bumpy, there is a mechanism to protect their capital.

The investor is the driver. You decide where the car goes, how fast, and whether the trip is worth taking at all.

A seatbelt does not make the road safe — it makes a crash survivable. Likewise, lender approval does not make an investment inherently good. It simply means the lender believes they will get repaid.

Practical Takeaways

1. Never rely solely on lender approval as your investment green light.

2. Learn how lenders stress test deals and use that discipline in your own underwriting.

3. Study loan covenants — they are a window into the deal's risk profile.

4. Prioritize your own goals, not just the lender's comfort level.

A Brief Memory from a Conversation with Rossi

Jane once recalled Rossi telling her over coffee:

> "Jane, a lender's job is not to make you rich. It is to make sure they do not lose money. Sometimes those goals align, sometimes they do not. Your job is to know the difference."

It was a simple truth, but one Jane carried into every deal review thereafter.

Now that you understand how lender priorities align with — and diverge from — your own, it is time to examine the **specific metrics** lenders use to size and monitor loans. In the next section, we will break down **Debt Service Coverage Ratio (DSCR)**, **Debt Yield (DY)**, and **Loan-to-Value (LTV)**, so you can interpret them with the same clarity a lender does.

Key Loan Metrics from A Lender's Angle: DSCR, Debt Yield, LTV

Why These Three Ratios Matter Most to Lenders

In the world of multifamily financing, lenders have dozens of data points at their disposal. But three ratios dominate their decision-making: **Debt Service Coverage Ratio (DSCR)**, **Debt Yield (DY)**, and **Loan-to-Value (LTV)**.

From a lender's perspective, these metrics are not just numbers — they are guardrails that protect their capital. They reveal whether the property generates enough income to cover the loan, whether the loan size is reasonable for the income it produces, and whether the collateral is worth more than the debt it secures.

An investor who understands these ratios as a lender does gains an advantage: the ability to spot risk through the same lens the loan committee uses.

1. Debt Service Coverage Ratio (DSCR) – The Cash Flow Gatekeeper

Definition:

DSCR measures a property's net operating income (NOI) relative to its total debt service (principal + interest payments).

Formula:

DSCR = NOI ÷ Debt Service

Why Lenders Care:

For lenders, DSCR is the first and most important test of whether a property's income can cover loan payments comfortably. A DSCR below the minimum covenant signals insufficient buffer, making the loan too risky.

Typical Lender Thresholds:

- Common minimum: 1.25x–1.30x for stabilized assets.

- Higher minimums (1.35x–1.50x) for higher-risk profiles — such as transitional properties, weaker borrowers, or markets with economic volatility.

How Lenders Really Use It:

- They run **base case** and **downside case** DSCR scenarios, adjusting rent growth down and expenses up to test covenant compliance.

- They check both **Year 1 DSCR** and projected DSCR over the loan term.

- They may define DSCR differently in the loan agreement — for example, using adjusted NOI, excluding certain income, or calculating against imputed principal in interest-only periods.

Investor Takeaway:

Do not assume the lender's DSCR threshold matches your comfort zone and ensure you know the lender's definition of DSCR for covenant compliance purposes. An investor may want a higher DSCR buffer than the lender requires, especially if relying on early cash flow.

2. Debt Yield (DY) – The Risk Compass

Definition:

Debt Yield = NOI ÷ Loan Amount.

It is a pure measure of how much income the property generates relative to the size of the loan, independent of interest rates or amortization.

Why Lenders Care:

Debt yield answers a simple question: *If we had to take over the property, how quickly could we recover our principal from operations (operating cash flow)?*

A 10% debt yield means it would take roughly 10 years of NOI to repay the loan in full. Lower yields mean higher leverage and greater risk.

Typical Lender Thresholds:

- Many lenders target a **minimum of 10%** for stabilized assets.
- Lower thresholds may apply for premier assets in prime locations with strong borrowers, but in volatile markets, the bar rises.

How Lenders Really Use It:

- As a **loan sizing tool** when interest rates are low and DSCR is less telling.
- As an ongoing **covenant test** in some credit agreements.

- To monitor risk over time — a declining debt yield after loan closing can trigger re-margin provisions or increased scrutiny.

Investor Takeaway:

A healthy debt yield means more breathing room for the lender — and for you. If the lender sizes your loan down due to low debt yield, that is a signal the deal may be over-leveraged for your comfort too.

3. Loan-to-Value (LTV) – The Collateral Cushion

Definition:

LTV = Loan Amount ÷ Appraised Value.

Why Lenders Care:

LTV tells the lender how much of the property's value is being financed. A lower LTV means more equity in the deal — their safety net if they have to foreclose.

Typical Lender Thresholds:

- 65%–75% for most stabilized multifamily loans (in a down market like the one in 2022-2025, it is not uncommon to see 50-60% LTVs).

- Lower maximums (60%–65%) for higher-risk markets, assets in weaker condition, or non-recourse structures.

How Lenders Really Use It:

- As a **final check** after DSCR and debt yield pass.

- To balance the other metrics — if DSCR and DY are strong, lenders may allow a slightly higher LTV.

- In combination with the borrower's net worth and liquidity to assess overall repayment strength.

Investor Takeaway:

While LTV is a useful snapshot, it does not determine loan proceeds. Cash flow does. Lower leverage protects not only the lender's position in a liquidation, but also your own principal and returns.

How Lenders Prioritize These Metrics Together

Think of these three metrics as a tripod: DSCR, Debt Yield, and LTV all support the lender's risk decision. If one leg is weak, the others must be stronger to compensate.

For example:

- **High DSCR + High Debt Yield + High LTV:** Lender might still approve if borrower strength is exceptional.

- **Low Debt Yield + Adequate DSCR:** Loan size may be reduced to meet the lender's minimum DY.

- **Adequate DSCR + Adequate DY + High LTV:** Possible if market and borrower are strong, but pricing may be less favorable.

A Brief Rossi Insight

In one of Jane's early mentorship calls, Rossi summed it up:

> "These three ratios are a lender's heartbeat. If one of them falters, the whole credit decision shifts. Learn to think in DSCR, DY, and LTV, and you will hear the lender's pulse before they even speak."

Jane later realized that by running her own DSCR, debt yield, and LTV checks — the way a lender would — she could predict how much leverage a deal would realistically support, often before the sponsor shared the term sheet.

Practical Steps for Investors

1. **Calculate All Three Early** – Run DSCR, DY, and LTV before diving into the full underwriting.

2. **Test Against Lender Standards** – Use conservative thresholds to see if the deal would pass lender sizing.

3. **Align Debt Structure with Investment Goals** – Do not just meet lender minimums; build in your own safety margin.

4. **Watch for Covenant Clues** – If a lender sets unusually high DSCR or DY thresholds, that is a direct signal they see higher risk.

Now that you understand the three core lending metrics and why they matter so much to the bank's credit committee, the next step is to see **how the lending process actually works from application to approval** — and how you can position yourself to negotiate the best terms possible.

The Lending Process from Application to Approval

Why the Lending Process Matters for Investors

For most multifamily acquisitions, debt covers 60%–75% of the purchase price. That means the lender is the largest single capital partner in the deal — and their approval is critical to closing.

From the lender's side, the process from application to approval is designed to answer one fundamental question: *Can this borrower, with this property, repay this loan in full, on time, under the agreed terms?*

Understanding this process from their perspective helps you anticipate requirements, avoid delays, and position yourself for better terms.

Stage 1: Pre-Application — Setting the Stage

Before a formal loan application, there is often a **pre-screen** or **initial conversation** between the borrower (or their mortgage broker) and the lender.

Lender's Focus at This Stage:

- Quick assessment of borrower profile: track record, net worth, liquidity.
- Initial impression of the property: asset type, location, condition, and occupancy.
- Fit with the lender's target market and product type.

Investor Tip:

Have a concise "lender packet" ready — resume or track record, personal financial statement, deal summary, rent roll, trailing 12-month operating statement. This demonstrates professionalism and can fast-track interest.

Stage 2: Loan Application Submission

The formal application includes detailed information about:

- **Borrower/Guarantors:** Experience, credit history, liquidity, net worth.

- **Property:** Rent roll, trailing 12 months of income/ expenses, photos, market overview.

- **Business Plan:** Renovation scope, lease-up strategy, rent growth assumptions.

Lender's Focus at This Stage:

- Matching the request to an appropriate loan product (e.g., agency, bank, bridge, CMBS).

- Determining preliminary sizing based on DSCR, Debt Yield, and LTV.

- Spotting early red flags in the plan or financials.

Stage 3: Term Sheet / Loan Proposal

If the lender is interested, they issue a **term sheet** or **letter of intent** outlining key terms:

- Loan amount, interest rate, amortization, term length.

- Recourse vs. non-recourse provisions.

- Prepayment penalties, covenants, reporting requirements.

Lender's Perspective:

This is **not** yet a commitment — it is a framework for moving forward. The final terms can change after full underwriting and due diligence.

Investor Tip:

Review term sheets carefully. Pay attention to covenants, not just rate and proceeds. This is where "hidden" lender priorities show up — such as unusually high DSCR minimums or restrictive negative covenants.

Stage 4: Full Underwriting and Due Diligence

This is where the lender's work intensifies. Their credit team will:

- Order an appraisal, environmental report, and property condition assessment, among others.

- Reconstruct financials to their own standards (normalizing expenses, discounting certain income).

- Stress test DSCR, DY, and LTV under base case and downside scenarios.

- Review borrower personal financials and compliance with liquidity and net worth requirements.

Lender's Goal:

Validate collateral value, confirm sustainable cash flow, and ensure borrower strength.

Common Surprises for Borrowers:

- Lenders may reject parts of the pro forma and underwrite to lower rents or higher expenses.

- Certain income streams (e.g., RUBS, parking) may be discounted or excluded.

- Loan sizing can drop between application and final approval if new data emerges.

Stage 5: Credit Committee Review

The lender's credit committee is the final internal checkpoint (not all lenders go through this process — more on that in the next section). They will:

- Examine underwriting results and risk mitigants.

- Ensure the deal fits within portfolio risk limits (e.g., concentration by asset type or market).

- Confirm borrower relationship value — sometimes a strong history can tip a borderline deal into approval.

Investor Tip:

Strong pre-existing relationships with lenders make this stage smoother. A borrower with a record of transparency, timely reporting, and covenant compliance earns more trust — and often more flexibility.

Stage 6: Commitment Letter and Closing Preparation

If approved, the lender may issue a **commitment letter** (usually they do not but in some cases for super strong borrowers and special situations, they might) — a binding agreement to lend under specified terms, subject to any final conditions.

From here:

- Loan documents are drafted (credit agreement, mortgage/deed of trust, guarantees).

- Closing conditions are cleared (insurance certificates, final estoppels, equity funding proof).

- Funds are wired at closing, **if** due diligence comes back as initially expected with no material variances or surprises and **if** there are no unexpected market turns.

The Lender's Pet Peeves — and How to Avoid Them

Drawing from my lending experience, *Rossi added*, here are behaviors that frustrate lenders and slow down approvals:

- **Incomplete or delayed documentation** — slows every stage.

- **Surprises** — especially undisclosed changes in occupancy, expenses, or management.

- **Not reading loan documents** — leading to preventable covenant breaches.

- **Weak communication** — silence when an issue arises erodes trust.

Applying This Knowledge as an Investor

Even if you are a passive investor and not the one signing the loan, knowing the process helps you:

- Ask better questions of your operator.

- Interpret lender-imposed changes as signals about deal risk.

- Understand where delays or term changes are most likely to occur.

A Brief Rossi Reflection

Jane once asked Rossi why some deals seemed to sail through underwriting while others stalled for weeks. Rossi smiled and said:

> "It is not luck. It is preparation, transparency, and making the lender's job easy. If you are the kind of borrower a credit officer brags about in meetings, you will never struggle for financing."

Practical Takeaways

1. **Respect the process** — each stage has a purpose and its own timeline.

2. **Be proactive** — provide complete, accurate information before being asked.

3. **Anticipate lender concerns** — run your own stress tests before they do.

4. **Build relationships early** — do not wait until you need a loan to meet a lender.

With the process from application to approval now clear, the final piece in this bonus section is knowing **the right questions to ask your lender.** In the next section, we will explore how to dig deeper into loan terms, covenants, and conditions so you can protect your position and negotiate from strength.

Questions Every Investor Should Ask Their Lender

Why Asking Questions Is a Sign of Strength

Many borrowers, especially newer ones, treat the lending process as a one-way interview: the lender asks questions, and they answer. But experienced operators know the conversation works both ways.

From the lender's perspective, a borrower who asks thoughtful, specific questions demonstrates three things:

1. They understand the debt structure and the business risk.

2. They are proactive about compliance and performance.

3. They will be a more predictable, lower-maintenance client.

The right questions protect you from surprises, strengthen the lender relationship, and provide insight into how they are really viewing your deal.

1. What Is Your Minimum DSCR Requirement — and How Is It Defined?

Why This Matters:

Lenders can define Debt Service Coverage Ratio differently — adjusted NOI, exclusions for certain income, interest-only variations. The definition affects both loan sizing and covenant compliance.

Follow-Up:

- Ask how they calculate DSCR during interest-only periods.

- Clarify whether replacement reserves or capital expenditures (or other items) are deducted from NOI in their calculation.

- Confirm how often DSCR will be tested post-closing and what triggers a breach.

2. Do You Have a Minimum Debt Yield or Re-Margin Requirement?

Why This Matters:

Debt Yield is often the hidden deal killer. If NOI ÷ Loan Amount falls below their threshold, your loan amount could be cut regardless of DSCR.

Follow-Up:

- Ask what minimum applies for your asset class and market.

- Confirm whether Debt Yield will be monitored after closing.
- If there is a covenant, ask what remedies are available if the property falls short such as a re-margin requirement, which effectively means paying down the loan so it fits a certain leverage (LTV) or debt yield profile.

3. What Maximum LTV Will You Allow for This Deal?

Why This Matters:

Loan-to-Value limits set the collateral cushion for the lender. Higher LTV can mean higher perceived risk.

Follow-Up:

- Ask how they determine value — appraised value, purchase price, or the lower of the two.
- Clarify if LTV is measured only at closing or if they reserve the right to re-measure later (e.g., during refinances or modifications or material market fluctuations).

4. What Are the Key Negative Covenants I Need to Watch?

Why This Matters:

Negative covenants restrict certain actions — changing property management, taking on additional debt, or making certain distributions. Breaching them can trigger defaults even if loan payments are current.

Follow-Up:

- Ask if shareholder loans require prior approval and whether they must be subordinated.

- Clarify the process for requesting exceptions.

- Find out how quickly the lender responds to modification requests.

5. How Will You Stress Test the Deal?

Why This Matters:

Lenders run base-case and downside-case scenarios. Knowing their stress test assumptions helps you understand their risk view.

Follow-Up:

- Ask what rent growth, vacancy, and expense assumptions they will use.

- Confirm if they adjust capital expenditure timelines in the downside case.

- Use these insights to align your own conservative case.

6. What Reporting Will You Require — and How Often?

Why This Matters:

Lenders often require periodic rent rolls, operating statements, insurance certificates, and personal financial statements. Missing a reporting deadline can be a performance default.

Follow-Up:

- Ask for a sample reporting calendar.

- Clarify if they allow electronic submissions.

- Confirm whether reports go to a dedicated portfolio or relationship manager or a rotating/centralized servicing team.

7. What Are the Prepayment Penalties or Exit Costs?

Why This Matters:

Yield maintenance, defeasance, and step-down penalties can dramatically affect your ability to refinance or sell early.

Follow-Up:

- Ask how penalties are calculated in dollars, not just formulas.

- Confirm if penalties apply to partial prepayments.

- If the loan has a lockout period, ask when you can start a payoff discussion.

8. How Do You View the Market for This Asset?

Why This Matters:

Lenders have internal research and portfolio data that can give you early insight into how professionals perceive your market's risks and strengths.

Follow-Up:

- Ask if they are seeing underwriting tighten in your market.

- Find out if their loan committee has special conditions for properties there.

9. If Something Goes Wrong, How Do You Typically Handle It?

Why This Matters:

Not all lenders handle distress the same way. Some work proactively with borrowers; others move quickly to enforce remedies.

Follow-Up:

- Ask for examples of how they have worked with borrowers in the past.

- Find out who would be your primary contact in a workout situation as well as who the credit approvers and key decision makers are.

10. What Could Make This Loan Unattractive to You Between Now and Closing?

Why This Matters:

Conditions can change during underwriting. Knowing the lender's deal-breakers helps you manage risk until funding.

Follow-Up:

- Ask if they have concentration limits by market, asset type, or borrower exposure (and ideally find out if you may be impacted by such).

- Clarify whether material occupancy drops or rent roll changes could trigger a re-price or decline.

A Brief Rossi Observation

Rossi once told Jane,

> "You can tell a lot about a lender by how they answer your questions. If they are defensive or vague, take note — transparency goes both ways."

Jane learned that the quality of answers often mattered as much as the answers themselves.

Practical Takeaways

1. **Ask before you sign** — the best time to clarify terms is before commitment, not after closing.

2. **Document answers** — keep a record of all commitments and clarifications for future reference.

3. **Use answers to sharpen your own underwriting** — if a lender is uneasy about an assumption, you should be too.

By now, you have seen how lenders think, the metrics they use, the process they follow, and the questions that reveal their true comfort level with your deal.

The takeaway is simple: lenders are partners with a different priority set. Learn their language, anticipate their concerns, and you will not only secure better financing — you will make stronger, more resilient investment decisions.

CHAPTER 10 [BONUS CHAPTER 2]

FEES, WATERFALLS, AND KEY PPM SECTIONS

Understanding GP and LP Roles

The Confusion in the Fine Print

Jane remembered sitting at her kitchen table, flipping through a hundred-page Private Placement Memorandum. She had already signed the subscription agreement for her first multifamily deal, but as she looked back, one phrase stood out — *"Class A Members (Limited Partners)"* on one page, *"Class B Members (General Partners)"* on another.

At the time, those labels might as well have been in another language.

During one of her mentorship sessions with Rossi, she admitted, "I knew I was an investor, but I never really stopped to think — what exactly am I in this deal? What am I entitled to, and what am I not?"

Rossi smiled and replied, "Understanding who you are in a deal — GP or LP — is the foundation for knowing how you make money, how decisions get made, and how much risk you carry. If you do not know that, the rest of the PPM might as well be a foreign novel."

This is where many investors start — focusing on the property, the returns, and the marketing pitch without first clarifying their actual role in the business. Once you know whether you are a General Partner or a Limited Partner, everything else — fees, waterfalls, voting rights, and even tax allocations — comes into sharper focus.

The Two Pillars of a Syndication

A real estate syndication is essentially a partnership between two main groups:

- **General Partners (GPs)** — Also called "sponsors" or "operators," they find, acquire, finance, and manage the property.

- **Limited Partners (LPs)** — Also called "passive investors" or "members," they contribute most of the capital and share in the profits, but do not manage day-to-day operations.

Think of it like a commercial flight. The GPs are in the cockpit — navigating the flight plan, responding to turbulence, and making sure the plane lands safely. The LPs are in the cabin — they have purchased a ticket, they expect to reach the destination, and while they do not control the flight, they still have the right to know how the trip is going and if any major detours are happening.

General Partner (GP) — The Active Manager

Core Responsibilities

The GP team wears many hats:

- **Deal sourcing** – Reviewing dozens or even hundreds of opportunities before selecting one that meets the strategy.

- **Due diligence** – Ordering inspections, reviewing leases, negotiating contracts, and stress-testing projections.

- **Capital raising** – Securing both debt from lenders and equity from investors.

- **Business plan execution** – Managing renovations, overseeing the property manager, adjusting strategy based on performance.

- **Compliance and reporting** – Sending investor updates, producing financial reports, filing K-1 tax forms, and staying within SEC and lender requirements.

- **Disposition** – Managing the sale process to maximize returns and taking care of post-sale items such as closing the books, issuing the final tax returns/K1s, etc.

Compensation

GPs are typically compensated through:

- A portion of the equity (often 20–30% of profits after the LPs receive their preferred return).

- Various fees (which we will break down in the next section).

- Their own LP-style investment if they co-invest personal capital.

Risks and Accountability

GPs bear significant operational risk. If the business plan is poorly executed or the property underperforms, the GP's compensation — especially the profit share — suffers. In some cases, a GP or its principals may also personally guarantee debt, putting their personal balance sheet on the line.

Limited Partner (LP) — The Passive Owner

Core Responsibilities

LPs provide the majority of the equity needed to close the deal. Beyond wiring funds and reviewing periodic updates, their involvement is intentionally limited to none in day-to-day operations. They do not:

- Hire or fire property managers.

- Approve vendor contracts.

- Decide when to refinance or sell (unless granted specific voting rights).

Compensation

LPs typically receive:

- A preferred return (e.g., 6–8% annually) — paid before GPs receive profit distributions. [Note: Not all investment offerings are structured to include a preferred return.]

- A pro rata share of remaining profits after the preferred return is met.

- Proceeds from the sale or refinance, according to the deal's waterfall structure.

Risks and Protections

An LP's liability is generally limited to the amount they invest — hence the name. However, they are still exposed to market risk, operational mismanagement, and financing challenges. If the deal falters, distributions can be paused, capital calls initiated, and in worst cases, principal lost.

The PPM as the Map of Roles

In every syndication, the Private Placement Memorandum (PPM) and Operating Agreement spell out GP and LP roles with legal precision:

- **Ownership splits** – Often 70% LP / 30% GP, but variations exist.

- **Voting rights** – Usually limited for LPs, but may be triggered in special circumstances (e.g., replacing the manager).

- **Monetary rights** – Details on preferred returns, profit splits, and how fees are paid before distributions.

- **Transfer and redemption rules** – Whether and how LPs can sell or transfer their shares.

If there is ever a question about "who can do what," the PPM is the rulebook. And as Rossi told Jane, "If you sign without reading and understanding it, you are not investing — you are gambling."

Real-World Scenarios

1. The Silent Investor Surprise

An LP assumed she could vote on a mid-hold refinance because she contributed 10% of the total equity. The PPM made it clear that only the GP could make that decision. She had influence only in very narrow "extraordinary event" cases — none of which applied.

Lesson: LPs must verify their actual decision-making rights before investing.

2. The GP Who "Invested" as an LP

In one deal, the GP team invested only a portion of their acquisition fee and no other capital as an LP in the deal. This meant they had very little skin in the game (cash out of pocket) in the deal.

Lesson: A GP's "skin in the game" can be a positive signal — but only if it is meaningful relative to the deal size.

3. The Preferred Equity Twist

Some deals include a third party: a preferred equity partner. This investor sits between the lender and common equity (LPs) in the capital stack. They may have veto power over major decisions and require higher priority payouts, which can dilute LP returns.

Lesson: LPs must understand *all* players in the stack, not just GP and LP roles.

Insider Warnings from the Field

1. **Do not assume "partner" means "equal say."** In most deals, LPs are passive by design.

2. **Watch for GP role overlap.** In vertically integrated companies, the GP may also own the property management company, construction firm, or broker. This can create conflicts if not transparently managed.

3. **Know the exit triggers.** Some operating agreements allow LPs to remove the GP for cause; others make it nearly impossible.

4. **Check capital call provisions.** Optional capital calls may cause ownership dilution for non-participants; mandatory calls are rare but binding.

5. **Confirm GP's ongoing responsibilities post-close.** Some sponsors outsource asset management — which is not necessarily bad, but you should know who is watching the store.

The Power of Clarity

When Jane finally understood GP and LP roles, she told me, "It was like someone handed me the keys to the room where all the real decisions are made. I might not sit at the table as an LP, but I now know exactly who does — and what motivates them."

Knowing your role is not about inflating or diminishing your importance. It is about aligning expectations, understanding your rights, and being realistic about your influence over the deal's direction.

Your Role in the Bigger Picture

Before you look at a deal's projected returns, first ask:

- Am I being offered a GP or LP position?

- What are the exact rights and responsibilities of that role?

- How are decisions made, and by whom?

- How do profits flow to me in this role?

Once you have those answers, every fee, waterfall, and risk factor in the PPM becomes easier to decode. You are no longer trying to read a foreign language — you are reading a contract that defines your place in the investment.

Whether you are taking the controls as a GP or investing from the cabin as an LP, clarity is your best protection and your best advantage. The most successful investors I know never gloss over role definitions — they start there. And once you know exactly who you are in the deal, you can move to the next critical question: *How is each party compensated?* That is where we go next.

Common Fees in Multifamily Deals — and Their Impact

The First Time Jane Looked Past the Headline Returns

In her early investing days, Jane used to scan the glossy investment deck until she reached the page with projected returns. That was the number she wanted — annual cash-on-cash, IRR, equity multiple.

Then, during her mentorship program, she recalled Rossi asking a single question that stopped her cold:

"Do you know how much the GP is getting paid before you see a dime?"

Rossi had her open the Private Placement Memorandum to the "Fees and Compensation" section. They walked through each line item — not just what it was called, but what it meant for her bottom line. She told Rossi later, "I realized I had been agreeing to terms I never really read."

Fees are not inherently bad. In fact, they are essential to compensate GPs for the substantial time, capital, and risk they take on. But as a Limited Partner, you need to know:

- Which fees are charged?
- When they are charged.
- How much is reasonable.
- How they align (or misalign) incentives.

Why Fees Matter

Every dollar in fees comes from the property's cash flow or from the capital you invest. If fees are excessive or poorly structured, they can erode returns for LPs. Conversely, well-structured fees reward GPs for performance and align their incentives with yours.

A fee review should never be a quick glance at percentages. It should be a reasonableness check against industry norms, the deal's complexity, and the GP's actual workload.

Acquisition Fee

What It Is:

A one-time fee paid to the GP at closing, usually a percentage of the purchase price. It compensates the GP for sourcing, underwriting, negotiating, and closing the deal — often after reviewing dozens of properties and incurring upfront costs (travel, inspections, deposits lost on deals they walk away from) as well as the front-end work of sourcing loan options, negotiating terms, and coordinating with lenders.

Typical Range: 2–5% of the purchase price.

Reasonableness Check:

- **Green zone:** 1–3% for larger deals; 3–5% for smaller or more complex transactions.

- **Yellow flag:** Above 5% without compelling justification.

- **Red flag:** High fee plus other large upfront charges — may signal GP is more focused on transactions than long-term performance.

Investor Tip: Ask whether the GP is rolling some or all of this fee back into the deal. While not required, it can show alignment (especially if they are not contributing additional capital to the deal).

Asset Management Fee

What It Is:

An ongoing fee, usually 1–2% of effective gross income or net operating income, paid for overseeing the property manager, tracking performance against the business plan, and making operational decisions.

Typical Range: 2% of collected income.

Reasonableness Check:

- **Green zone:** 2% of collected income (EGI).

- **Yellow flag:** Above 2%, especially if the GP's role is light-touch. If based on NOI (vs. EGI), a higher fee of 4-5% is not uncommon.

- **Red flag:** Fee based on *equity raised* instead of property income — this misaligns incentives because it pays regardless of performance.

Investor Tip: Confirm whether the GP continues to collect this fee if distributions are paused. Some will, some will not.

Construction or Renovation Management Fee

What It Is:

A fee, often 5–10% of the renovation budget, paid to the GP for managing capital improvement projects. This can include contractor oversight, permitting, and ensuring the work aligns with the value-add plan.

Typical Range: 5% of rehab budget; could be up to 10% for heavier lift and larger renovations/capex.

Reasonableness Check:

- **Green zone:** Fee tied to actual renovation scope and progress.

- **Yellow flag:** Full fee charged upfront for minimal rehab work.

- **Red flag:** Duplicate charges if GP also owns the construction company doing the work — unless disclosed and competitively bid.

Investor Tip: Tie fee payments to project milestones, not just the capital budget.

Financing or Refinance Fee

What It Is:

A fee, typically 0.5–2% of the loan amount, paid when securing financing or refinancing. It is typically a pass-through fee charged by the loan broker or lender but may include a spread to compensate the GP for managing the loan refi process, which would include soliciting proposals, evaluating and selecting the optimal refi terms, working with the lender and property manager to provide the needed information to complete the refi, and coordinating post-close activities related to returning of capital to the LPs.

Typical Range:

- Acquisition financing: 1–2% of loan amount.

- Refinance: 0.5–1% of loan amount.

Reasonableness Check:

- **Green zone:** Within ranges above, with clear scope of work.

- **Yellow flag:** Charged when GP did not materially participate in the loan process.

- **Red flag:** Charged on top of the loan broker/lender finance/refinance fees noted above.

Loan Guarantee Fee

What It Is:

Paid to a guarantor who pledges personal assets to secure the loan.

Typical Range: 1-2% of the loan amount.

Reasonableness Check:

- **Green zone:** Within range, especially when personal balance sheet risk is real.

- **Yellow flag:** Full fee charged but guarantee risk is minimal.

- **Red flag:** No disclosure of guarantor's identity or their relationship to the GP.

Investor Tip: If the guarantor is part of the GP team, understand if this is in addition to their GP compensation.

Disposition Fee

What It Is:

Paid at sale (1–2% of sale price) for preparing the property for market, coordinating with brokers, and managing closing.

Typical Range: 1–2% of sale price.

Reasonableness Check:

- **Green zone:** Fee tied to actual sales execution.
- **Yellow flag:** Fee charged when GP does little beyond hiring a broker.
- **Red flag:** Fee stacked with a separate broker commission without explanation or fee stacked along a 3%+ acquisition fee (if a disposition fee is charged on the back end, the acquisition fee on the front end is usually lower). Fee paid, even if the deal underperforms or capital is lost.

Other Possible Fees

- **Organization and Offering Costs:** Typically capped at a reasonable dollar amount or percentage. Should be tied to legal, accounting, and marketing costs of setting up the syndication.

- **Capital Event Fee:** Charged upon cash-out refinance or supplemental loan. Should be modest (often 1% of proceeds).

- **Property Management Fee:** If GP owns the property management company, confirm if the rate is market-competitive.

How Fees Affect Returns

Fees reduce distributable cash to LPs — directly if they come from operations, or indirectly if they are paid from capital raises. The more front-loaded the fees, the more cautious you should be. A deal with high acquisition and construction fees may leave the GP financially comfortable even if the property underperforms.

On the other hand, a deal with modest upfront fees and performance-based profit sharing ties the GP's upside to yours.

Jane's Turning Point

Rossi once gave Jane an exercise: take a deal proforma and strip away all the fees. Then, add them back one by one, watching how each impacted LP returns.

Jane's takeaway was simple: "A deal that looked like a home run on paper could be an average performer after fees — and a poor one if the business plan slips."

She learned to treat the fee section of the PPM as seriously as the rent roll or expense budget. "Now," she said, "I cannot imagine wiring money without knowing exactly what the GP earns and why."

Your Fee Review Checklist

Before you invest, ask:

1. What fees are being charged? List them all.

2. Are they within industry norms?

3. Are they paid from operations, capital, or at closing?

4. Do they align GP incentives with LP performance?

5. Are they clearly disclosed in the PPM?

If the answers do not sit well with you, it is a sign to pause.

Understanding fees is not about nickel-and-diming the GP (after all you want the GP to be well compensated and therefore incentivized to not only perform but outperform the deal or alternatively to manage the deal and protect the principal during stormy days). It is about making sure you are entering a partnership where both sides win when the business plan succeeds. The next step is to understand how profits are shared — which brings us to **Waterfall Structures Explained in Plain English**, where we will decode exactly how money flows from the property to your bank account.

Waterfall Structures Explained in Plain English

The Napkin Diagram That Changed Everything

Jane still laughs about the first time Rossi explained a waterfall to her.

They were at a small café after a property tour. Rossi grabbed a napkin, drew a vertical line down the middle, and began sketching boxes and arrows.

"Money in real estate deals flows like a waterfall," she said. "The property generates cash flow, and that money cascades through a series of steps — one tier fills before the next gets a drop. Your job is to know exactly where you stand in that flow."

At the time, Jane thought it was just a cute analogy. But as she began investing in more deals, she realized that knowing the waterfall was not just about understanding when she got paid — it was about understanding how *much* she got paid, and how the GP's incentives lined up with hers.

What a Waterfall Is — and Why It Matters

In multifamily syndications, the "waterfall" is the sequence in which available cash flow is distributed to investors and the GP. There are cash flow waterfalls and capital event waterfalls. It dictates:

- **Order of payment** – who gets paid first, second, third, and so on.

- **How much each tier receives** – based on return rates, capital contributions, and profit splits.

- **When splits change** – often after hitting certain performance targets ("hurdles").

Think of the waterfall as the property's financial plumbing. If it is designed well, everyone benefits when the business plan succeeds. If it is poorly designed, the GP could win big while LPs are left with lower-than-expected returns — even if the property performs.

The Foundation: Preferred Return

The **preferred return** ("pref") is a target return that LPs receive *before* GPs participate in profit sharing. Not all deals are structured with a pref.

- **Typical Range:** 6–8% annually.

- **Purpose:** Gives LPs priority in cash flow distributions, compensating them for providing capital and taking on risk.

- **Types:**

  - **Cumulative:** If the property does not generate enough cash to pay the full pref in a given year, the shortfall rolls forward.

  - **Cumulative & Compounding:** Same as above, but the pref is calculated on the accrued amount (vs. the initial principal investment amount) — more favorable to LPs.

  - **Non-cumulative:** Unpaid amounts are lost — least favorable for LPs.

LP Watchpoint: Always check if the pref is based on **unreturned capital** (returns diminish as capital is returned) or **total original investment** (better for LPs).

Return of Capital vs. Return on Capital

This detail often hides in the PPM's fine print but has major implications:

- **Return on Capital:** Distributions do not reduce your capital balance, so your pref is calculated on the full amount you originally invested until your principal is returned at sale or refinance.

- **Return of Capital:** Distributions reduce your capital balance, so the pref is calculated on a shrinking base — meaning smaller future payments.

LP Watchpoint: Return on capital is generally more favorable. If it is return of capital, project future cash flows to see how quickly your pref will shrink.

Profit Splits — The Heart of the Waterfall

After the pref is satisfied, remaining cash is split between LPs and GPs according to the ownership structure.

- **Common Split:** 70% LP / 30% GP.

- **Performance Hurdles:** In some deals, this split changes once the GP achieves a certain internal rate of return (IRR), equity multiple, or average annual return (AAR).

Example:

- Tier 1: 8% pref to LPs.

- Tier 2: Remaining profits split 70% LP / 30% GP until GP hits 20% IRR.

- Tier 3: Profits above a 20% IRR, split 50% LP / 50% GP.

This "promote" rewards GPs for exceeding performance targets — but LPs should ensure the hurdles are meaningful and realistic.

Cash Flow vs. Capital Waterfalls

Cash Flow Waterfall:

1. Pay pref to LPs (if deal is structured with a pref).

2. Split remaining profits according to ownership percentage.

Capital Event Waterfall:

1. Pay off the loan and other liabilities.

2. Pay transaction fees associated with the sale or refinance.

3. Pay accrued but unpaid pref to LPs (cumulative or cumulative & compounding).

4. Return LP capital (the initial principal amount).

5. Split profits (or if a deal is structured with hurdles, then split profits at one rate until hurdle achieved and adjust split at higher rate for GP after hurdle, as documented in the PPM).

Tiered waterfalls can align incentives — or, if poorly designed, accelerate GP upside too early.

The Hidden Risks in Waterfalls

1. **Unrealistic Hurdles:** If the hurdle is so high it is never achieved, the GP may have no incentive to outperform after hitting the pref.

2. **Early Promote:** Triggers tied to metrics that can be met before real value is created.

3. **Non-cumulative Prefs:** LPs permanently lose unpaid returns in weak years.

4. **Return of Capital Treatment:** Shrinks future pref payments without obvious warning.

5. **Cash Flow Timing:** Delayed distributions may affect your liquidity even if IRR looks healthy.

Jane's Waterfall Moment

In one mentorship session, Rossi had Jane draw a waterfall for a real deal she was considering. She quickly realized that while the marketing deck highlighted an "8% preferred return," the PPM revealed it was *non-cumulative* and calculated on **returned** capital.

Her actual cash flow, if the business plan slipped even slightly, could be much lower than advertised. She passed on the deal.

"That napkin exercise," she told me later, "probably saved me from a mediocre investment disguised as a great one."

Your Waterfall Review Checklist

Before investing:

1. **Identify the preferred return:** Is it cumulative? Compounding? Non-cumulative?

2. **Clarify capital treatment:** Return on or return of?

3. **Map out profit splits:** What are the LP/GP percentages in each tier?

4. **Check hurdle triggers:** Which metric is used — IRR, AAR, equity multiple — and is it meaningful?

5. **Model timing:** When are distributions expected, and how do they affect your cash flow needs?

Once you understand the waterfall, you no longer just look at projected returns — you understand exactly *how* those returns get to you, and what needs to happen for the GP to get their share. That level of clarity protects you from surprises and positions you to ask sharper questions before you invest.

With GP/LP roles, fees, and waterfalls now clear, the next step is to put it all together by knowing where the biggest risks hide in the PPM.

PPM Red Flags Every Investor Should Spot

The Night Jane Learned to Read the Fine Print

Jane once told Rossi about the first time she really *read* a Private Placement Memorandum (PPM).

It was during her mentorship program. She had brought Rossi a deal she was excited about — strong market, reasonable leverage, conservative rent growth assumptions. On paper, it looked solid.

They sat down together to review it, as Jane slid the PPM across the table. "Tonight," Rossi said, "we are going to read the part no one talks about in webinars."

An hour later, Jane looked up in disbelief. Buried deep in the operating agreement was a mandatory capital call provision. Not optional. Not capped. If the GP requested additional capital, every investor was legally required to contribute or face losing their ownership stake entirely.

"That," Rossi told her, "Is why you never sign without reading — and understanding — the fine print."

Why the PPM Matters

In a syndication, the PPM (and specifically the Operating Agreement within the PPM) is not just a formality — it is the **rulebook** for the deal. The marketing deck may show you projected returns and beautiful property photos, but the PPM is where the binding terms live.

It spells out:

- How and when money flows (distributions, waterfalls, fees).

- What rights you have as an investor.

- What rights you do not have.

- How disputes are resolved.

- What happens in extreme scenarios (capital calls, GP removal, forced sales).

If a conflict arises, the PPM — not the glossy deck — governs. As Rossi likes to say, "The PPM is the deal. Everything else is marketing."

The Top Red Flag Zones in a PPM

1. Capital Call Provisions

A capital call occurs when the GP requests additional funds after closing. This might be due to unexpected expenses, cost overruns, or a downturn that strains cash flow.

- **Optional Participation:** LPs can choose to contribute. Non-participants may see their ownership diluted.

- **Mandatory Participation:** LPs must contribute or risk incurring both penalties and severe dilution.

Red Flag: Mandatory calls with no cap, unclear consequences, or penalties beyond dilution.

LP Action: Ask the GP how often they have done capital calls and under what circumstances. Review whether they have adequate reserves to reduce the likelihood.

2. Distribution and Preferred Return Language

We covered waterfalls earlier, but here is the key: the PPM is where the legal version lives.

- Is the preferred return **cumulative** or **non-cumulative**?

- Is it **compounding**?

- Is it based on **return on capital** or **return of capital**?

- How frequently are **distributions** paid?

Red Flag: Vague or undefined pref terms, or clauses that allow the GP to change distribution timing "at their discretion" without limits.

LP Action: Confirm terms match the marketing materials — and if they do not, the PPM wins.

3. Fee Structure and Payment Priority

Every fee the GP earns should be clearly spelled out — including when it is paid and from what source.

Red Flag:

- Asset management fees based on equity raised rather than performance (misaligned incentives).

- Stacked fees (e.g., GP owns the property management company and charges **above-market** rates without disclosure).

- Large upfront fees that are paid regardless of future performance.

LP Action: Compare fee terms to industry norms and ensure they are in line with what you reviewed in the investment summary.

4. Voting Powers and GP Removal

Most LPs have limited voting rights, but some events trigger the need for investor approval — such as removing a GP for cause or approving a major change in strategy.

Red Flag: GP removal provisions that require an unrealistically high percentage of LP votes (e.g., unanimous consent). This can make it nearly impossible to remove a GP even in cases of negligence (as GPs are often LPs in their own deals, i.e., invest in their own deals).

LP Action: Check the exact threshold required for removal and what qualifies as "for cause."

5. Transfer and Redemption Restrictions

Syndication investments are illiquid, but the PPM should specify whether — and how — you can sell or transfer your interest (if at all).

Red Flag:

- Redemption rights that are vague or undefined.

LP Action: Know your exit options before you invest — even if you plan to hold until sale.

6. Risk Factors

This section is usually long and intimidating — sometimes dozens of pages. Many investors skip it, but it is worth at least a careful scan.

Red Flag: Missing or glossed-over risks. If the property is in a hurricane zone but there is no mention of storm risk, that is a problem.

LP Action: Compare risks disclosed to the property's location, condition, and business plan. If something is missing, ask the GP to explain why.

How to Review a PPM Without Feeling Overwhelmed

1. **Start with the Table of Contents** – Find capital call provisions, fee schedules, waterfalls, and distribution terms quickly.

2. **Cross-check with the investment summary** – Any mismatch defaults to the PPM.

3. **Highlight "at discretion" language** – This is where flexibility can turn into risk.

4. **Look for numbers, not just words** – Percentages, thresholds, and caps matter.

5. **Ask the GP for clarification in writing** – Keep a paper trail.

Jane's PPM Confidence Moment

Months after that first deep dive, Jane brought Rossi another deal. This time, she had marked up the PPM with sticky notes and questions.

"Capital calls optional. Pref is cumulative, return on capital, 8%. GP removal requires a 75% vote. All fees disclosed and reasonable," she said without looking at her notes.

She smiled. "I think I am starting to speak PPM."

The PPM is not bedtime reading, but it is your primary shield against unwanted surprises. Once you know where the red flags hide, you stop being a passive participant in your own investment decisions. You become an informed partner — one who understands not just the potential rewards, but the rules of the game.

With GP and LP roles clear, fees understood, waterfalls decoded, and PPM red flags on your radar, you now have the full toolkit to assess a multifamily deal with confidence — and the discipline to walk away when the fine print tells a different story than the pitch.

PPM Mastery Challenge: For your next investment opportunity, spend one hour focused solely on the PPM sections covered in this chapter. Create a simple scorecard: Green (acceptable), Yellow (concerning), Red (deal-breaker). Do not invest unless you have mostly greens and can explain every yellow. Remember: the PPM is the deal, everything else is marketing.

CHAPTER 11

YOUR FIRST (OR NEXT) CONFIDENT DEAL

Preparing Your Investment Criteria Checklist and Running Your Own Underwriting from Start to Finish

Why Your Criteria Matter More Than the Deal in Front of You

Every investor has experienced the tug of temptation when a glossy pitch deck lands in their inbox. The photos gleam, the projected returns sparkle, and the story about a "fast-growing market" feels like it was written just for you. This is where discipline either saves you — or costs you dearly.

If you have no clear investment criteria, you will be pulled into the gravity of someone else's vision. You will start justifying weak fundamentals because the rent comps "look close enough," or because the sponsor has an impressive track record. The problem is, without a personal compass, you are navigating by someone else's stars.

This chapter is about building that compass. By the end, you will have a written, non-negotiable investment criteria checklist — your decision-making filter that turns deal evaluation from an emotional reaction into a structured process. This is the first step to becoming the kind of investor who can pass on ninety percent of deals with zero fear of missing out, knowing the remaining ten percent will fit your goals, your risk tolerance, and your standards.

The Role of the Checklist in Your Journey

Up to now, you have learned how to analyze income, expenses, reserves, debt structure, and cap rates using the five-step underwriting framework discussed in Chapter 6. You have seen how lenders think, and you have learned to spot overly optimistic assumptions. You have the tools — but tools need a blueprint to follow.

Your checklist will:

- Clarify what you will and will not accept in a deal.

- Keep you from "falling in love" with a property before you see the numbers.

- Help you make fast, confident decisions without second-guessing.

- Protect you from shiny-object syndrome and sponsor hype.

When Jane reached this stage under Rossi's mentorship, she finally stopped thinking like a "reactive" investor and started thinking like a "selective" one. Rossi told her, "If you do not set your rules before the deal shows up, the deal will set the rules for you." That single sentence became Jane's investing mantra.

Defining Your Personal Investment Goals

Before you can write down your criteria, you need to anchor them to your bigger picture. Ask yourself:

1. **What is the primary purpose of your investments right now?**

   - Income today (cash flow).

   - Long-term appreciation.

   - Tax advantages.

   - A mix, with a priority order.

2. **What is your target hold period?**

   - Are you comfortable with a 7–10-year hold, or do you prefer shorter timelines?

3. **What level of involvement do you want?**

   - Purely passive with trusted sponsors.

   - More active review and involvement in decision-making.

4. **What is your personal risk tolerance?**

   - Can you handle short-term volatility if the long-term upside is strong?

   - Do you prefer a steady, predictable income stream?

Defining these anchors now prevents you from saying "yes" to a deal that looks exciting but does not fit the financial life you are building.

Translating Goals into Hard Criteria

Here is where your checklist starts to take shape. We are going to convert your broad goals into measurable thresholds. Think of this as turning "I want strong cash flow" into "Minimum 6% annualized average cash-on-cash return."

Market & Demographics:

- Median household income ≥ $50,000.

- Rent-to-income ratio below 33%.

- Positive job and population growth over the last 3 years.

- Industry diversity — no single employer responsible for more than 20% of jobs.

Property Fundamentals:

- Asset class B or better (unless you have a deliberate strategy for C-class value-add and understand the risks).

- In a neighborhood with low violent crime rates.

- Strong demand indicators — cost to own at least $500 higher than cost to rent.

Deal Structure:

- Purchase cap rate at or above current market cap rate.

- Exit cap rate at least 50 bps higher than purchase, if it is a five-year hold deal (unless in a proven high-growth market).

- Leverage capped at 70% LTV, including any preferred equity.

- Fixed-rate debt preferred; if floating, must have a rate cap in place.

Operations & Underwriting:

- Minimum 6 months of operating expense reserves.

- Year-1 rent growth assumption ≤ current market trend (often 0% in a softer market).

- Realistic expense ratio ≥ 45% of EGI and ≥ $6,000 per door annually to reflect minimum line-item expenses for R&M, turns, admin, marketing, and contract services and tax and insurance adjustments, as discussed in earlier chapters.

- No exit cap rate compression.

Projected Returns:

- Cash-on-cash return: ≥ 6% average.

- Equity multiple: ≥ 1.8x over the hold period.

- IRR: ≥ 15% with conservative assumptions.

- Break-even occupancy of 70% or less and no more than 80%.

These categories and numbers are examples — yours may be tighter or looser depending on your experience, market focus, and goals. The key is that they are defined in advance.

Addressing Common Mental Blocks

Many new investors hesitate to create hard criteria because they fear they will "miss out" on a great deal. The fact of the matter is: discipline in deal selection does not limit opportunities; it filters for the right ones.

If you find yourself thinking:

- "What if a slightly weaker deal ends up being amazing?" — remember, your goal is not to catch every fish, it is to catch the fish you want to eat.

- "I am not an underwriter — can I really trust my own criteria?" — you are not replacing sponsor analysis; you are cross-checking it for alignment with your own standards.

Rossi often reminded Jane, "Numbers can be dressed up like a storefront window. Your criteria are the glass you see through, not the reflection someone wants you to see."

Building Your Checklist Step by Step

Step 1 — Brain Dump:

Write down every quality or metric you think matters in a deal. Do not worry about formatting — just list them as they come.

Step 2 — Categorize:

Sort them into groups: Market, Property, Deal Structure, Operations, Returns.

Step 3 — Set Thresholds:

Wherever possible, assign a specific number or definition. For example, instead of "low crime," define "crime rate below city average for violent incidents."

Step 4 — Prioritize:

Decide which criteria are "non-negotiable" and which are "strong preferences." Non-negotiables should be bolded in your final checklist.

Step 5 — Format for Use:

Keep it to one-three pages. You want something you can quickly reference when reviewing a new opportunity.

How to Use Your Checklist in Real Life

The moment you receive a deal, run it through your checklist before opening the underwriting model. This does two things:

1. **Saves Time:** If it fails on non-negotiables (for example, in a stagnant job market or in a high-crime area), you can move on immediately.

2. **Removes Emotion:** You are deciding based on pre-set standards, not on the sponsor's excitement or the property photos.

When Jane adopted this habit, she noticed an immediate change. She stopped spending hours on deals that never had a chance of meeting her goals. Her confidence rose because every "no" felt like a deliberate, strategic choice — not a missed opportunity.

Integrating Lender Discipline into Your Criteria

One of the strongest advantages you have now is the lender's perspective you learned in earlier chapters. Lenders protect their capital by stress-testing deals — and you can do the same.

Ask yourself:

- If I were lending my own money on this deal, would I be comfortable with the risk profile?

- Does the DSCR hold up if income drops by 5%?

- Can the deal survive 12 months of flat rent growth without eating into reserves?

If your answer is "no" to any of these, the deal is not for you — regardless of how good it looks on paper.

Maintaining and Updating Your Checklist

Your criteria are not carved in stone. As you gain experience, markets shift, or your life stages change, you may adjust them. The key is to make changes **deliberately**, not in the heat of a tempting opportunity.

Set a reminder to review your checklist quarterly or whenever a major market shift occurs. Keep track of deals you passed on and why — this will help you see patterns and refine your criteria.

The Mindset Shift This Creates

Writing down your investment criteria changes how you see deals. You are no longer chasing someone else's definition of a "good" investment. You have your own. You stop measuring success by the number of deals you close and start measuring it by the quality of the deals you choose.

Jane summed it up best after passing on a flashy, over-leveraged project in a "hot" market: "For the first time, I felt like I was the one interviewing the deal, not the other way around."

Your investment criteria checklist is more than a document — it is a declaration of independence. It says, "I know what I am looking for, and I will not compromise my standards for the sake of being in a deal." With it, you are not at the mercy of market noise, sponsor persuasion, or investor chatter. You are guided by your own clear, tested principles.

Your Workflow for Running Underwriting (After You Vet The Operator and The Market)

1. **Initial Filter:** Apply your checklist to rule out clear misfits.

2. **Five-Step Framework (after vetting the market):** Income → Expenses → Reserves → Debt → Cap Rates/ Pro Forma Valuation.

3. **Stress Testing:** Apply lender-style downside scenarios.

4. **Decision Prep:** Summarize findings against your non-negotiables and preferences.

5. **Bonus:** Understand the fee and waterfall structure in a deal and review the PPM.

<u>Tip:</u> Keep a digital or printed template of your process so you can run it the same way every time. Consistency is what makes your analysis reliable.

Why This Matters for Your First Confident Deal

When you follow this sequence, you remove the guesswork. You no longer chase numbers you hope are true; you reveal the numbers that are most likely to hold up in reality.

Rossi summed it up for Jane after her first full underwriting: "Deals do not win you over — they pass your test. That is how you protect your capital and your peace of mind."

You now have the ability to take any multifamily deal from a glossy marketing package to a fully vetted investment decision. You are no longer an audience member in the investing world; you are in the driver's seat. In the next section, you will take the final step — turning your underwriting into a definitive choice: yes, no, or wait. That moment, more than any spreadsheet, is where you claim your identity as a confident, risk-smart investor.

Making the Decision — Yes, No, or Wait

The Decision Point

Underwriting is not an academic exercise. Its purpose is to lead you to a clear, confident decision: invest now, decline, or monitor the opportunity for a future entry. This is where you bridge analysis and action.

At this point, you have:

- Applied your investment criteria checklist.
- Run the full five-step underwriting framework.
- Stress-tested the deal as a lender would.

Now you must weigh your findings against your goals and risk tolerance.

Rossi told Jane early on, "Underwriting without a decision is like buying all the ingredients but never cooking the meal." This chapter ensures you leave the kitchen with a finished dish — one you are proud to serve yourself.

Yes — When the Deal Passes Your Tests

A "yes" deal is not a perfect deal. It is a deal that:

- Meets or exceeds all non-negotiable criteria.

- Holds up under conservative assumptions.

- Fits your broader portfolio strategy.

- Offers a risk profile you can live with, even if projections come in slightly under.

Before giving a yes:

- Review the sponsor's track record again for alignment and trustworthiness.

- Reconfirm financing terms in writing.

- Make sure you understand the business plan in detail — including exit strategy.

Jane's first yes came when she found a property in a submarket with steady job growth, conservative rent growth projections, a seasoned operator, and fixed-rate debt. It was not flashy, but it was sound — and she could sleep at night knowing her capital was well-positioned.

No — When the Deal Fails Your Standards

A "no" is often easier than a "yes" because the red flags are clear:

- Multiple non-negotiables missed.

- High sensitivity to minor market shifts.

- Aggressive financing with limited reserves.

The discipline is in saying no without regret. Remember: declining a deal is a positive action — it is an investment in capital preservation.

Jane passed on several deals that, on paper, had higher projected returns than her eventual first yes. She realized those returns were based on best-case scenarios that had little chance of materializing.

Wait — When Timing or Conditions Are Not Right

Sometimes a deal is strong in fundamentals but missing one or two elements that could change. This is where "wait" comes in.

Example:

- The market is currently oversupplied, but absorption is projected to improve in 12 months.

- Financing terms could improve with a rate environment shift.

A "wait" is only effective if you set a clear recheck timeline and know exactly what conditions you are monitoring.

Decision Framework

To simplify:

1. **Meets all non-negotiables?** If no, decline.

2. **Stress-tested performance still acceptable?** If no, decline.

3. **Sponsor and market confidence strong?** If yes, proceed.

4. **Minor gaps that could change?** If yes, consider wait.

Your decision should fit on one page. If you need paragraphs to justify a yes, you might be forcing it.

Saying yes, no, or wait with confidence is the mark of a disciplined investor. You are no longer swayed by hype or paralyzed by uncertainty — you act on evidence, aligned with your strategy.

The Emotional Side of Your First Confident Yes

Why This Moment Matters

Your first confident yes is more than a transaction. It is the culmination of the journey from uncertainty to clarity, from relying on others to relying on yourself. It is proof that you can evaluate, decide, and commit — all without second-guessing.

Jane described the feeling as "quiet excitement." Not the adrenaline rush of chasing something shiny, but the calm assurance that comes from knowing she had vetted every angle and could defend her choice to anyone — including herself.

Balancing Excitement with Discipline

When you say yes, your natural excitement can tempt you to relax your standards for the next deal. This is where you must remember: discipline is a habit, not a one-time event.

Rossi warned Jane: "Your next yes must earn its place the same way this one did." That reminder kept her from slipping into complacency.

Navigating Post-Commitment Jitters

Even with a confident yes, it is normal to feel flickers of doubt before wiring funds. You might find yourself replaying "what if" scenarios or imagining market downturns.

To manage this:

- Revisit your underwriting summary — remind yourself why the deal passed your standards.

- Focus on factors within your control (due diligence, ongoing monitoring) and release what you cannot control (macroeconomic shifts).

- Keep a journal of your decision process; it will build trust in your future choices.

The Ripple Effect of a Confident Yes

The first yes is a foundation. It shapes how you approach every subsequent deal and how others perceive you as an investor. You become the person who does not chase — you choose.

Jane noticed sponsors treated her differently after she asked precise, criteria-driven questions. Her reputation shifted from "interested" to "informed," which opened doors to higher-quality opportunities.

Your first confident yes is not the end of the journey — it is the turning point where your identity as a savvy, risk-aware investor is cemented. From here, every deal you evaluate will be seen through the lens of the skills, discipline, and self-trust you have built. And that, more than any single investment, is what will build your long-term success.

HOW THE STORY ENDS

Jane could see it clearly now — the arc of her journey from that gut-punch morning when the foreclosure email shattered her confidence, to the quiet certainty she felt today. She had turned fear into faith, both in herself and in the possibility of a better future. What had once been seen as failure was now the foundation on which she stood, stronger and wiser.

She knew she could not have done it alone. Rossi's mentorship had been more than guidance; it was the steady hand that kept her on course when the seas were rough. Through every spreadsheet, every late-night question, and every "look again" moment, Rossi had helped her grow into an educated, empowered investor — one who could meet the market with clarity instead of anxiety.

Jane remembered Rossi's words, spoken over coffee on a morning much like this one: *"The sun always shines brighter and stronger after the storm."*

Stepping outside, she felt that truth on her skin. The air was crisp, the sky a wide expanse of blue. She took a slow sip of her coffee, set it down, and began her morning jog. The sun was warm on her face, and with each step, she felt the steady rhythm of someone who had found her footing — not just in investing, but in herself.

APPENDIX A
CONTINUING THE JOURNEY

Mastering the fundamentals of underwriting is not the end of your path — it is the beginning. The skills you have learned will serve you for years to come, but the market will keep changing, and every deal will bring new nuances to consider. The most successful investors keep their tools sharp, their minds open, and their network strong.

This final section is your bridge from the page to practice. It is where you take what you have learned here and integrate it into your real-world investing life — with support, structure, and resources designed to keep you moving forward with clarity and confidence.

Your Underwriting Toolkit and Checklists

Every confident decision begins with a process you can trust.

To help you stay consistent, I have created the **Underwriting Toolkit**, which includes:

- The complete 5-Step Underwriting Framework in a single-page format for quick reference.

- Detailed checklists for income, expenses, reserves, debt, and cap rate analysis.

- A quick-screening worksheet to filter opportunities in minutes.

You can access the full toolkit instantly by visiting the resources page that comes with this book, where you can download it for free (visit www.MasteringMultifamilyUnderwriting.com/book-resources).

Templates for Market, Deal, and Operator Vetting

The numbers tell one part of the story — but markets, deals, and operators each have their own unique risk profile.

To help you evaluate them thoroughly, I have included three complementary templates:

1. **Market Vetting Template** – Identify growth trends, affordability, and stability before committing to a location.

2. **Deal Vetting Template** – Capture all assumptions in one place, making it easier to spot unrealistic projections.

3. **Operator Vetting Template** – Guide your conversations with sponsors and uncover their track record, strategy, and risk management practices.

These templates are available via the same resource page: www.MasteringMultifamilyUnderwriting.com/book-resources.

Resources for Ongoing Skill Development

Underwriting is a skill that grows sharper with repetition and exposure to new scenarios. To keep you progressing:

- **Mastering Multifamily Underwriting (MMU) Community and Self-Paced Course** – You will find a curated set of video lessons, case studies, and tools to deepen your understanding of multifamily analysis. We meet monthly and you can enjoy additional content, guides, weekly posts to keep your underwriting acumen sharp.

- **Bonus One-on-One Session** – As a thank-you for reading to the end, upon enrollment in MMU or joining the community, you will receive an additional **complimentary 60-minute one on one consult call**. The promo code is "Book". The bonus call can be utilized for any additional questions you have, or a second set of eyes on a deal, or anything related to multifamily underwriting and deal analysis you need a sounding board on.

You will be provided with the booking link upon enrollment. Make sure you mention the promo code above.

Staying Sharp: Practice, Review, and Community

Even the most skilled investors benefit from peer feedback and shared learning. Consider building or joining a community of like-minded investors who:

- Share deals and underwriting notes for discussion.

- Compare market research and operator insights.

- Hold each other accountable to disciplined decision-making.

The resources page will also connect you to opportunities to join our private community, where you can exchange knowledge and build relationships with other serious investors.

Your Next Step

Close this book knowing that you have the knowledge, the tools, and the discipline to make investment decisions you can stand behind. Now, it is time to put that into action. Access your toolkit, download your templates, claim your bonus call, and join a community that will help you stay sharp for years to come visit: www.MasteringMultifamilyUnderwriting. com/book-resources).

Because the best investors are not those who start with all the answers — they are the ones who keep learning, keep asking, and keep showing up prepared for every opportunity.

APPENDIX B

GLOSSARY OF KEY TERMS

Acquisition Fee (2-5% of purchase price) – typically paid to the General Partners (GPs) at the close. However, in some scenarios, some GPs may choose to invest the proceeds in the deal or may delay collection of the fee until a certain Limited Partner (LP) return is achieved. GPs would often review many deals before they find the one where the numbers make sense. This process will often entail additional expenses, such as travel, earnest money deposits gone hard on a deal they ultimately chose to walk away from, diligence reports/reviews on a deal that did not move forward, etc. The acquisition fee partially compensates GPs for that effort and the aforementioned out-of-pocket costs.

Additional collateral support typically includes personal guarantees from the sponsors or key principals. Some lenders (agencies) may also have certain requirements, e.g. the guarantor(s) must possess (combined) liquidity (cash and marketable securities) equal to a minimum of 10% of the loan amount and (combined) net worth equal to the loan amount. When the loan requires a personal guarantee, it is also known as recourse loan.

Amortization/Amort

Debt amortization is the process of paying off a loan through scheduled, pre-determined installments that include principal and interest.

For example: 30-yr straight line amortization on a 300,000 loan would equate to annual principal payment of $10,000. Based on that schedule, the loan would be fully paid off in 30 years.

Average Annual Return (AAR)

Return **on** investment *averaged over the hold period of the asset*, measured as total cash flow distribution to members throughout the tenor of the deal plus the capital gain at the time of sale <u>divided by</u> the principal amount <u>divided by</u> the hold period.

Example:

Initial investment amount: $100,000.
Total cash distributions and capital gain received at the time of sale: $100,000.
Hold period: 5 years.
AAR is calculated as follows -
($100,000 profit /$100,000 principal amount) / 5 years = 20% AAR

Asset Management Fee (1-2% of effective gross or of net income) – typically paid out of the monthly cash flow. It compensates the GP for the time and effort involved in actively managing the asset to ensure execution against the original business plan progresses as scheduled.

Basis points (bps)

Equals 1/100 of 1%.

Examples: 10 bps = 0.10%; 25 bps = 0.25%; 50 bps = 0.50%, 100 bps = 1%, etc.

Break-Even Occupancy

Calculated as total operating expenses plus debt service divided by <u>effective gross income</u>.

Measures at what point of occupancy revenue generated by the property covers the property expenses (including debt service) just enough to break even.

May see that measured as both unit count and %.

A break-even of 80-unit count on a 100-unit property for example, simply means that occupancy can decrease from 100 to 80 units before it breaks even.

Similarly, a break-even of 80% simply means economic occupancy can drop to 80% before the property breaks even.

Capital Expenditures (Capex)

The amount spent on improving a property.

An example would be: replacing roofs, updating electrical, painting the building, updating interior units.

It is best that the capex reserves are raised for upfront and NOT relying on cash flow from operations to fund capex.

Cap Rate

The rate of return on a real estate investment property based on the income such property generates/is expected to generate AND if purchased all cash.

Factors affecting the cap rate:

- underlying economic or market conditions
- interest rates
- demand for and supply of the underlying asset
- asset class
- location
- building age and condition, etc.

Usually, the higher the risk profile of the asset, the higher the expected cap rate will be. Think higher risk – higher return.

Where to find market cap rate – broker reports, CoStar, appraisals, being active in the market, apartmentloanstore. com

Cap rate compression means cap rates are decreasing, i.e. values are rising.

Cap rate reversion (decompression) means cap rates are increasing, i.e. values are declining.

Entry Cap Rate or Purchase Price Cap Rate = Actual (in-place) NOI at time of purchase/ Purchase Price.

Exit Cap Rate = Actual (in-place) NOI at time of sale/ Sale Price.

Market Cap Rate = cap rate at which properties are trading at in the market today.

Cash Flow After Debt Service/CAPEX/AM Fees

Usually shows that net profit (NOI) after Debt Service, Capex, and Other fees (e.g. asset management fees).

Cash flow available for distributions is NOI less Debt Service less Asset Management Fee. If capex is not reserved for upfront, then capex also needs to be subtracted from the number above to determine the amount of distributable cash.

Cash On Cash Return (CoC)

Cash income earned relative to the original cash investment. The original cash investment typically includes the down payment on a loan (if the property is financed), closing costs, capex reserves, and operating reserves.

For example, a property generating $10,000 in annual cash flow after debt service and initial cash investment of $100,000, has a 10% cash on cash return.

Closing costs and fees, including exit fees

These are the typical fees required for diligence and processing the transaction and may include but not limited to: appraisal/environmental/seismic/property condition reports, underwriting fees, lender legal fees, title and title insurance fees, escrow, etc.

Collateral

This is the asset that you pledge to secure the loan. In the event of foreclosure, the lender can step in and sell the asset in order to fully or partially pay off the loan balance and eliminate or reduce their losses, respectively. Sometimes a lender may require the owner to cross collateralize certain properties (usually if the subject asset is in a more distressed position). When cross collateralizing properties be careful because you are typically not allowed to pledge properties that are already encumbered by another lender. In addition, if the subject property fails, you are at risk or losing the cross-collateralized properties too.

Construction Management Fee (5-10% of rehab budget) – for properties that may require more work to turn around in a short period of time, it serves to compensate the GP during that transition period for managing contractors, leasing efforts, and the property manager.

Contract Rent: The Rent is the rent being charged and collected on existing leases at a property. In contrast to Market Rent, contract rent is not based on market conditions but rather is based on the lease contract signed between the landlord and tenant.

Core (Class A) Properties that are: Built in the last 10-15 years. The highest quality. Modern construction. Lowest amount of deferred maintenance. Premium and several amenities (gym, dog park, office, community room, pool, spa, etc.). In excellent locations, good school districts, high income-low crime areas. Tenant base is white collar or high income.

Command the highest rent. More sensitive to recessions; tenant base may transition to a Class B property during a recession. A higher purchase price, lower cash on cash return, lower but more stable cash flows, and the greatest potential for appreciation, lowest level of risk. Cap rates tend to be the lowest.

Core Plus (Class B) Properties that are: Built in the last 15-30 years. Construction is generally of good quality. May be brought up to a Class B+ or Class A level after substantial renovation and modernization. Opportunity for forced appreciation via value-add updates. Some deferred maintenance. Fewer amenities. Located in stable neighborhoods and moderate income and low to moderate crime areas. The tenant base is a mix of middle-income professionals and higher earning blue collar workers. Rents are moderate. Less expensive than Class A properties. Moderate cash on cash return, moderate cap rate, moderate to high appreciation and moderate risk.

Covenant structure

To monitor loan performance and establish early triggers in the event of property deterioration, most lenders would have loan covenants (financial and reporting). The most typical financial covenant is a minimum DSCR. The most typical reporting requirements are the annual operating statement, rent roll as well as any other reports required from the loan guarantor, if the loan is recourse-based. Some lenders (typically the agencies) will also have opening requirements like min property occupancy of 90% for the 90 days preceding close, cap on tenant concentrations, etc.

Debt Service

The amount spent to service the debt. Usually the sum of the principal and interest. For interest only loans, it is the sum of interest.

Debt Service Coverage Ratio (DSCR)

The Annual NOI divided by Debt Service. Lenders usually require a minimum of 1.25x. Effectively it measures ability of the cash flow generated by the property (NOI) to service the debt (debt service).

Debt Yield

Debt yield is calculated as NOI divided by the loan amount. In essence, it represents the inverse of the property's cash flow leverage position. Lenders may apply this as they determine the loan size.

Disposition Fee (1-2% of the sale price) – typically paid at close/sale. It compensates the GP for the work put into preparing the property for sale and coordinating the sale to completion.

Economic Vacancy

The amount of occupied but non-paying units. Examples include – concessions, bad debt, employee units, etc.

Effective Gross Income

Equivalent to Net Revenue. Represents the gross income minus physical & economic vacancy plus other income.

Effective Rent

Actual rent charged, after concessions and discounts. Could also be referenced as in-place rent but should not be confused with contract rent (defined above).

Equity Multiple (EM)

Measured as total dollars received divided by total dollars invested. Total dollars received includes the cash flow earned throughout the hold period of the asset coupled with the sale proceeds.

For example, if you invested $100,000 and you received a total of $200,000 throughout the hold period of the asset including gain on sale and return of your principal, that means you achieved equity multiple of 2.00x or in other words you doubled your initial investment.

Garden Style Apartment

Garden-style apartments are low-rise, spread-out communities with outdoor entrances and landscaped settings, designed to feel more residential and less urban.

Gross Potential Rent

The maximum potential rent one can charge based on current market. May also be labeled as "market rent" on the T12.

Guarantor Fee (1-2% of the loan amount) – typically paid at close and designed to compensate the guarantor for putting up their personal balance sheet behind the deal. The guarantor may or may not choose to be involved in the day-to-day operations.

Therefore, they would want to be extra comfortable with the operators' ability to execute before signing the dotted line with their name. If the deal was to go bad, their name would be on the line.

Internal Rate of Return (IRR)

IRR is the discount rate that makes the net present value (NPV) of all cash flows equal to zero. In other words, it's the expected compound annual rate of return that will be earned on a project or investment. It captures the time value of money.

Less meaningful metric for forever buy and hold projects (CoC may be a better KPI for such projects).

Interest Only (IO)

The period during which the loan does NOT amortize and incurs only interest payments due.

Interest rate

The interest rate on the loan can be fixed (for part or the entire loan tenor) or floating (usually based on an Index like SOFR, BSBY, Prime, etc. plus a loan spread). If you choose a floating rate but are looking for ways to hedge the risk of rising interest rates you can use financial derivatives like swaps (a swap fixes the index rate) or options (collars (set a rate floor and a rate cap) or caps (set a cap on how high the index rate can increase)) to mitigate such risk. Banks may have capabilities to offer both swaps and options. Other loan providers may only be able to offer only options.

Investment Offering Memo

The investment offering is prepared by the lead sponsor team and details the investment opportunity. It is a marketing document (often referred to as pitch deck). It outlines the team, the market, the property, the financials aspects of the deal (including fees and projected returns), key risks, sensitivity analysis, and how to join the investment. The official investment is typically documented via the Private Placement Memorandum (PPM).

KPI = Key Performance Indicator

Loan Assumption

When one operator assumes the loan of another upon takeover of the property.

Key Considerations When Evaluating A Loan Assumption

- Sponsor strength
- Loan balance
- Loan tenor
- Loan amortization
- Interest-only period remaining, if any
- Interest rate, fixed or floating
- Min DSC
- Loan assumption fees
- Negotiate a discount when you are doing the seller a favor – e.g. assuming a higher rate loan

- Beware of the exit cap rate assumptions (especially when assuming a low interest rate loan in a higher cap rate environment)
- Usually, a 1% loan assumption fee is assessed by the lender

Loan Broker Fee (1-2% of the loan amount) – typically paid at close and designed to compensate the mortgage broker for the work put in to solicit the best financing terms and position the deal for success to the ultimate lender.

Loan sizing

While LTV is most commonly cited in prelim term sheets as a loan sizing metric, lenders would typically size the loan based on cash flow. Therefore, it is not uncommon for lenders to size the loan on the *lesser of* LTV, DSC, and Debt Yield.

Loan To Value (LTV)

Calculated as the amount of the loan divided by the property value. Often referred to as leverage.

Example: Loan amount of $1.5MM and property value of $2.0MM, would result in LTV of 75%.

Loan providers

The usual loan providers in the commercial real estate space are banks, agencies (Fannie Mae and Freddie Mac), commercial mortgage-backed securities providers (CMBS), and insurance companies. They each have varying tolerance of risk and property type requirements; therefore, each will usually have varying loan structures.

Loan types

The two most typical loan structures are bridge (short term, 1-3 years) and permanent (aka perm 3+ years).

LOI (Letter of Intent)

A document that outlines the preliminary terms and basic framework of a potential deal or transaction before a formal, legally binding contract is created. It is usually non-binding and serves as a roadmap for future negotiations, helping to streamline discussions and determine if the parties are aligned before committing to a final, formal agreement.

Loss/Gain to Lease

The difference between the maximum potential market rent and actual rent.

Loss to Lease indicates there is additional potential to increase rent.

Gain to Lease indicates, we are leasing at above market rates.

Market Rent

Usually listed on the rent roll. Indicates the market (typical/comp) rent for that particular unit type and size. It does not represent the maximum potential rent necessarily.

Mill

A "mill" is 1/1,000 of a dollar, or $1 for each $1,000 of assessed value. A mill is used to calculate a property's millage rate.

Millage Rate

The millage rate is used to calculate the property tax on real property. This is calculated in increments of $1,000, with each mill representing 0.1% of the property's taxed assessed value, which is often lower than market value. For example, if a property's tax assessed value is $20,000,000 and has a millage rate of 20, then its property tax would equate to $400,000 ($20 for every $1,000 of value). In many jurisdictions, the millage rate is converted to a percentage (mill rate ÷ 1000) and quoted as a property tax rate for ease of calculation.

Mortgage Constant

A rate calculated by dividing the periodic loan payment by the initial loan amount. The Mortgage (or Loan) Constant is often used as a tool to efficiently calculate loan payments and is represented as a percentage. For instance, a mortgage loan with an annual payment of $16,000 and an initial loan balance of $250,000 has a Mortgage Constant of 6.40%. In an interest only loan, this metric would be the same as the interest rate where with an amortizing loan this would be different because there are principal payments included as well.

Net Absorption

In the case of for lease property, net absorption is the rate at which rentable area is leased up over a

period of time in a given market. The net absorption figure considers construction of new space, demolition of existing space and any additional vacancies during that period. It is often used to forecast demand and supply trends and is thus a key indicator for both property owners and developers, significantly influencing their pricing and timing decisions.

Net Operating Income (NOI)

Equivalent to Operating Income of a business. Effective Gross Income (Rent) minus Operating Expenses.

In-place NOI = actual NOI (this is what lenders underwrite to).

Stabilized NOI = NOI reached when the property is stabilized (e.g., at market vacancy and rents and optimized expenses).

Occupancy

The number of occupied units.

Occupancy %: Occupied units as % of Gross Rent. The inverse of vacancy %.

Offering Memo (OM)

The memo, usually prepared by a commercial broker, that presents the deal, the investment opportunity, the market, and brief financial overview of the property.

Operating Expenses (Opex)

The necessary and ordinary expenses incurred to operate the property.

Examples include: Admin, Advertising, Contract Services, Insurance, Labor, Legal, Property Management, Repair & Maintenance, Replacement Reserves (usually imposed by the lender), Tax, Turns, Utilities, etc.

Operating Expense (Opex) Ratio (OER)

Operating Expenses divided by Effective Gross Income.

Usually ranges from 35-60%. Could be as low as 35% for brand new properties OR 60%+ for older properties with deferred maintenance. Most common is 50%.

HOWEVER, the ratio varies by market and property.

Opportunistic (Class D): Properties that are described as war zones. The roughest properties one can encounter. Constructed in the last 30-100 years. Often in poor condition and plagued with much deferred maintenance. No amenities. Located in the roughest part of town marked with violence, drugs, and prostitution. The tenant base is low income and may have a criminal record. The least expensive and the most risky and as a result will offer the highest cash on cash return Cash flow may be volatile. Even if upgraded, based on the property location, they will rarely appreciate in value and essentially have no exit plan. They represent the highest level of risk.

Other Income

Additional income generated by the property.

Examples: Pet Rent, Utility Bill Back, Laundry, Late charges, Parking, Valet Trash, etc.

Passive Investor

Often also referred to as the Limited Partner or LP. The investor is providing the capital and relying on the operator/

lead sponsor/general partner (GP) to manage the investment with the goal and expectation for probably future profits.

Physical Vacancy

The amount of non-occupied/vacant units.

Positive/Negative Leverage

Positive Leverage: When cap rate (or YOC) exceeds the loan interest rate. In other words, when the unlevered return exceeds the cost of capital.

Example: Cap rate of 6.5%. All in interest rate of 6%.

Negative Leverage: When the cap rate (or YOC) is below the loan interest rate. In other words, when the unlevered return does NOT exceed the cost of capital.

Example: Cap rate of 5%. All in interest rate of 6%.

Positive leverage is a good prelim indicator of positive cash flow.

If leverage is negative, then it might be best to buy the property all cash (vs. finance).

Preferred Return

A profit distribution preference whereby profits, either from operations, sale, or refinance, are distributed to one class of equity before another until a certain rate of return on the initial investment is reached.

Typically calculated on an annual basis and on the principal amount invested.

Typically paid first before any profit splits (promote) kick in.

Preferred returns are not guaranteed and depend on the cash flow generated by the property. As such, it is important to understand how they are treated in the event there is a shortfall.

The most typical structure is cumulative, i.e., the preferred balance due, if unpaid, carries over into the next year. LPs may not receive the return as planned but will not lose on it (unless the overall investment suffers a loss). And if it keeps accumulating till sale, such cumulative preferred return accrued to the LPs will be typically paid fist (after the loan and associated transaction fees as well as the invested principal amount), followed by the LP's share of the gains, and lastly the GP's share of the gain.

Cumulative and compounding is another method, whereby the preferred return not only accumulates over time, but the rate is calculated on the accrued balance (vs. the original principal balance). This method is less common and certainly more beneficial for the LPs.

Preferred return may be calculated on returned or unreturned capital contribution principal amount. This is why it is important to understand whether distributions constitute return on capital (most common) or return of capital (less common).

Prepayment penalties

It is not uncommon for loans to have penalties if the loan is paid off prior to the maturity date. Penalties can be structured differently (defeasance, yield maintenance, step down, etc.). Thus, it is important to understand the prepayment penalty structure upfront.

Promote

This is typically an outsized share of the profits, payable once the investors have received back their entire initial capital contributions and achieved certain profit thresholds (i.e., preferred return).

Promote is also referred to as the promoted interest or carried interest. Refers to how the profit splits/share on a syndication are structured. For example, a 30% promote would typically mean that 70% of profits go to the limited partners (passive investors) and 30% of profits go to the general partners (sponsors, syndication team).

Refinance Fee (1-2% of the loan amount) – typically paid at the close of the refi. It compensates the GP for managing the loan refi process, which would include soliciting proposals, evaluating and selecting the optimal refi terms, working with the lender and property manager to provide the needed information to complete the refi, and coordinating post-close activities related to returning of capital to the LPs.

Re-margin provisions

This requirement is more typical for banks vs. agencies. It effectively may require the owner to pay down the loan to bring LTV or DY within a certain hurdle in a scenario where market values decline.

Ratio Utility Billing System (RUBS)

A method of calculating a resident's utility bill based on specific factors such as occupancy rate or apartment square footage and then billing the tenant for their share of utility use.

SOFR (Secured Overnight Finance Rate)

SOFR replaced LIBOR (London Interbank Offered Rate) after the LIBOR scandals and is now the market rate often used by banks and other financial institutions for lending purposes on US-Dollar denominated contracts. It fluctuates daily and can have various tenors – daily, 1-month, 3-month, 6-month. SOFR's cousins include: SONIA (for GBP denominated loans), €STR (Euro), TONA (Japanese Yen), SARRON (Swiss Franc), CORRA (Canadian Dollar), SORA (Singapore Dollar), and AONIA (Australian Dollar).

Sponsor

This is the lead syndicator, the key operator leading and controlling the deal. They are often referred to as the General Partner or GP. This is the person (or people) who are responsible for the sourcing, management, and the disposition of the deal. Passive investors (LPs) rely on the GP's efforts to generate possible profits from the investment.

Stabilization period

The period of time required to reposition the asset from the time of purchase to a steady eddy run rate. Typically, 24-36 months for larger (150+ unit) assets or 12-18 months for smaller assets (10-50 units).

Stabilized NOI

The NOI run rate reached after the property is stabilized, i.e., after the repositioning activities are completed.

Tax

When and how they are assessed can vary from county to county. They can be assessed at the point of sale (POS), annually, every 3-5 years, etc.

How they are assessed can vary from county to county - % of the purchase price, mileage rate based on assessed property value (usually measured as % of the original purchase price).

Tenor

The loan tenor is the loan maturity date. While it is not uncommon to have a 30-year tenor for residential loans (1-4 units), for most commercial real estate the tenor is shorter (3-10 years) leaving a balloon payment due at maturity. This is not something to panic about. In most cases, at maturity the owner would either refinance the property (thereby extending the tenor) or sell the property (thereby paying off the loan with the sale proceeds).

Value Add (Class C) Properties that are: Built within the last 30-50 years. Have average to low functionality, typically outdated and in need of remodel. Have much more deferred maintenance and limited (if any) amenities. Opportunity for forced appreciation. Located in lower income-moderate crime areas Opportunity may be found in Class C properties located in Class B areas.

Rental rates are low to moderate. The tenant base typically comprises of blue collar/working class households. Turnover and vacancy tend to be higher. Less expensive than Class B properties.

Offer higher cash on cash return, higher cash flow, low to moderate appreciation, and pose higher risk. Cap rates tend to be higher.

Yield On Cost

The unlevered rate of return on an asset based on the all-in cost.

Calculated as Stabilized NOI divided by the All-In Cost of a Property (Purchase Price + Capex + Closing Costs).

ACKNOWLEDGMENTS

I wish to thank the special people who shaped my path and inspired me to write this book:

- My late uncle, **Dimitar Kostov** — a published author and bold entrepreneur who defied the odds behind the Iron Curtain. His words, "Kamăk da stisnesh, voda da padne" ("May water come out when you squeeze a stone"), reminded me never to give up.

- **Roumi and Nasko Radenski** — for welcoming me with open arms during my first Christmas in the United States, for guiding me when I was at a crossroad, and for showing me what it means to be both a good citizen and a generous friend. Roumi's work at the Library of Congress and Nasko's legacy as a published author continue to inspire me.

Your lives and examples proved to me that anyone with a message to share and value to add can become an author. I am deeply grateful.

AUTHOR BIO

VESSI KAPOULIAN is the Founder of Dream Believe Achieve Capital Group, a real estate investment firm based in Los Angeles, CA.

Vessi helps high achieving professionals and business owners generate passive income streams and create tax efficiencies via well vetted cash flowing investments in commercial real estate.

Vessi's professional background includes 15+ years of commercial lending and business management experience. Vessi started her real estate journey as an investor in 2017. Today Vessi manages a large portfolio of investor real estate properties. She is also passively invested in a number of deals.

Her commercial lending experience has served her well in developing a conservative and analytical approach in assessing risk and investing prudently in real estate in order to maximize returns. Her business experience has helped develop a solutions-oriented and execution-focused approach, which has served well in asset managing her real estate portfolio.

Drawing on her unique blend of lending expertise and investing experience, Vessi helps new and seasoned investors master the art and science of apartment underwriting. She also consults passive investors to help them navigate through the complexities of the deal numbers and structure, offering documents, or capital call situations. Lastly, Vessi advises family offices and private companies on strategic investment due diligence, risk management, and governance structures - helping them safeguard capital, optimize decision-making, and build sustainable multi-generational wealth.

Vessi is active in various real estate professional networks and a frequent speaker at meet ups, conferences, and podcasts.

Vessi's mission is to (i) help other high achieving professionals secure their own financial freedom & create more optionality in their lives and (ii) to help create educated and empowered investors through her work.

Vessi has earned a Bachelor degree from the University of Arkansas and an MBA from Northwestern University.

Can You Help?

Thank You For Reading My Book!

I really appreciate all of your feedback, and I love hearing what you have to say.

Your input to make the next version of this book and future books better would help many.

Please leave me an honest review on Amazon letting me know what you thought of the book.

Thanks so much!

Vessi Kapoulian

www.ingramcontent.com/pod-product-compliance
Lightning Source LLC
Chambersburg PA
CBHW031958150726

47990CB00005B/1765